NOVEL EPICS

NOVEL EPICS

Gogol, Dostoevsky, and National Narrative

Frederick T. Griffiths
and
Stanley J. Rabinowitz

NORTHWESTERN UNIVERSITY PRESS
EVANSTON, ILLINOIS

Northwestern University Press
Evanston, Illinois 60201

Printed in the United States of America

Library of Congress Cataloging-in-Publication Data

Griffiths, Frederick T.
    Novel epics : Gogol, Dostoevsky, and national narrative / Fred-
erick T. Griffiths and Stanley J. Rabinowitz.
      p. cm. — (Series in Russian literature and theory)
    Includes bibliographical references.
    ISBN 0-8101-0900-X. — ISBN 0-8101-0901-8 (pbk.)
    1. Russian fiction—19th century—History and criticism.
2. Russian fiction—20th century—History and criticism. [1. Gogol´,
Nikolaĭ Vasil´evich, 1809–1852. Mertvye dushi. 2. Dostoyevsky,
Fyodor, 1821–1881. Brat´ia Karamazovy.]
    I. Rabinowitz, Stanley J. II. Title. III. Series.
PG3332.M43G7   1990
891.73´309—dc20   90-6947
                                                       CIP

FOR DALE PETERSON

CONTENTS

ACKNOWLEDGMENTS

The authors gratefully acknowledge the advice and encouragement of Hugh McLean during the long evolution of this book.

We would also like to thank Amherst College for supporting the project through leaves and research grants, and in particular Richard Fink, who as dean of the faculty, colleague, and friend has assisted this collaboration from its inception. Our thanks also to the staff of Frost Library, especially to Floyd Merritt and the Interlibrary Loan Department, for showing resourcefulness and good humor throughout, and to Betty Steele and the staff of the Academic Computer Center for years of heroic resilience. A large debt is owed to Sara Upton for innumerable deft assists in the preparation of the manuscript.

An earlier version of the discussion of Gogol's *Selected Passages from Correspondence with Friends* was presented at the conference "The Logos of Gogol: Poetics, Aesthetics, Metaphysics," held at Wesleyan University, April 9 and 10, 1988.

The following publishers have generously given permission to use extended quotations from copyrighted works:

. . . chashche poèty, razdelennye vremenem i prostranstvom, otvechayut drug drugu, kak otgoloski mezhdu utyosami; razvyazka "Iliada" khranitsya v "Komedii" Dante.

. . . separated by time and space, poets quite often answer each other like echoes among cliffs; the denouement of the Iliad *is given in Dante's* Comedy.

——V. F. Odoevsky, *Russian Nights* (1835)

EPIC AND NOVEL   1

Two Romes have fallen, but a third stands fast; a fourth there cannot be.

Rome, Byzantium, Moscow: through this prophecy the six-teenth-century monk Philotheus evades an old and still unan-swered question—does Russia belong in Europe?—by proclaim-ing a Europe that spiritually belongs to Russia and should look to Moscow as the true and final capital of a renascent Chris-tendom. For the Slavs to westernize has always seemed a com-promise of the otherness and unworldliness that set them apart and above. By the logic of Christianity, their very innocence as outsiders can also signify spiritual election. The conversion of Christendom's northern periphery to its center and capital recalls the miracles of the rejected rock as capstone, the carpenter's son as Messiah, the meek inheriting. Something good can come from Nazareth. Indeed, it is to the Nazareths that one must look to find the future, for the old capitals, Rome as well as Jerusalem, fall prey to worldly success. Philotheus suggests how Slavophiles might welcome the prospect of leading Europe rather than joining it.

Yet danger lurks in this proud calling, for the process of redeeming publicans and sinners entails large risks of joining their number. Already by Philotheus's day the West had seen millennia of conquerors, among them the Romans themselves, battling their way to cultural enslavement. Though politically subjected, the Greeks may have prevailed culturally, as Horace already suspected: "Graecia capta ferum victorem cepit et artes / intulit agresti Latio" ("Conquered Greece conquered her fierce victor and brought the arts into rustic Latium," *Epistles* 2.1.156–57). The statuesque marble Romanness of Rome was framed by sophisticates who spoke Greek among themselves; in the best circles, Russians after 1812 both celebrated and compromised their expulsion of foreign masters by still speaking French as they pursued their own increasingly Napoleonic ambitions. The inheriting meek lose their meekness. Basic to the project of constructing the third and final Rome, in Europe but not of it, was the paradox that the wall erected against European influence would have to be built with European bricks. Perhaps the bulwark could become Russian by being grander than any wall yet built.

In the fabrication of this national identity, novelists enjoyed influence rarely seen in Western letters since antiquity, the influence of prophets. Once Napoleon was beaten, writers in Russia sought to forge an independent literature that would not only celebrate the country's new status as a world power but also allow fallen Europe to read its own destiny. For prophets, the wit or sentimentality of the novel, the bourgeois fantasy that sold books in Paris or London, was no fit medium. While the novel in its materialism and privatization portrayed the spiritual fragmentation of the West, Russian writers aimed to take the genre beyond itself by making it something greater, more public, and more primary—in a word, by making it monumental, that is, epic. It is in precisely these terms that Belinsky, the father of Russian criticism, defined the status of the novel: "The epic of our time is the novel."[1] The Homeric tradition could liberate Russian writers from the confines of the European novel by providing terms to assert the magnitude of their subject, their magnificent calling, and the finality of their inherited spiritual authority.[2] The epic, to be sure, is as European as the novel but emerged from a Europe as yet uncorrupted by the Enlightenment and by industrialization, the Europe destined to renew itself on Russian soil. The novel might become Russian by being grander than anything yet written.

The turning points in the national history—1812 and 1917—did in fact inspire responses that pointedly surpassed and questioned the inherited terms of the European novel by invoking the tradition of classical epic. Boris Eikhenbaum has observed that in writing *War and Peace* Tolstoy used the form of Homeric epic to escape the confines of the English family novel,[3] and we have argued elsewhere that the structure of heroism in the work owes specific and extensive debts to the *Iliad* and the *Odyssey*.[4] Pasternak's much more oblique and melancholy response to the October Revolution in *Doctor Zhivago* invokes Virgil's troubled celebration of the Roman revolution in the *Aeneid*. Pasternak in some measure defines his position (and that of his generation) in the shadow of Tolstoy by thus recalling the burdens and achievements of Virgil in the shadow of Homer. He proposes that Moscow has in fact become the Third Rome, not a final and flourishing bastion of Christian orthodoxy but the capital of a totalitarian empire. Just as Rome's empire left the city "a flea market of borrowed gods and conquered peoples," so Soviet culture may be killing Russian.[5]

Tolstoy and Pasternak were writing within an established national literature, and it is not surprising that as they looked back over the decades to turning points like 1812 and 1917 they should suggest that their works be read beside texts like the *Iliad* and the *Aeneid* that were also centrally engaged in the forming of national identities. Gogol and Dostoevsky form another strand within the great tradition of the Russian novel, one in which any trace of classicism is unexpected. Both writers address Petersburg life in their earlier short stories, and Dostoevsky's debts to Gogol on this score are well understood.[6] But as they wrote their masterpieces, *Dead Souls* and *The Brothers*

Karamazov, they turned away from the capitals and from national watersheds, and presumably therefore from any shadows of the epic tradition.[7] Indeed, *Dead Souls* seems to deflate the high, laureate style by its mock-heroic account of unwonted excitements in the provincial village of N——, midway between somewhere and nowhere. It was in a similar turning aside from epic and playful dismissal of heroism that the novel got its start in modern literatures with Cervantes, Rabelais, Sterne, and Fielding. Yet in these other literatures epic, as inspiration or target for parody, tends to fall from sight after the first generation, while in Russia, as we have seen, it keeps coming back at the crucial points of national history. The concluding question of *Dead Souls*, "Whither Rus'?" is more serious in its implications than the preceding text has seemed to be in style, and Gogol came to see his narrative as the first canticle of a divine comedy. When Dostoevsky recalls Gogol's project, as in some measure he does in *The Brothers Karamazov*, he does so not merely to satirize but to continue it. Dostoevsky also came to view his novel as the first part of some Russian divine comedy. The question of "Whither Rus'?" rises beyond the hollow rhetoric of Dmitri's prosecutor to renew the quest for the Russian identity broadly and seriously and, as we shall argue, against the allusive background of Homer and the classical as well as the Christian origins of the European tradition. The Russian novel, unlike the European, did not invoke the epic tradition to set itself playfully apart before turning to other concerns, but rather to begin a dialogue that is most apparent in the most esteemed texts.

Before turning to Gogol and, more briefly, to Dostoevsky's reflections on the tradition that he inherited from Gogol, we shall need to consider the relationship between epics and novels and in particular the question of how novels can locate themselves within a tradition that is often argued to be antithetical to the very nature of the novel.

The Double Plot of Epic

Epic is not only older than the novel but has a much better memory. Debts within the more idiosyncratic and mutable range of the novel conceal themselves easily, but epic has from the first been preoccupied with its own genealogy. How Aeneas will inevitably launch Rome would have intrigued the ancient reader less than whether Virgil would master or be mastered by the incomparable Homer, whom he rivaled and recreated line by line. *Hoc opus, hic labor est.* Virgil is reputed to have said that it is easier to steal the club of Hercules than to lift one line from Homer (*Vita Donati* 46). His heroic terms are apposite: Aeneas's risks rank as nothing compared to Virgil's as heir and rival to Homer. The *Aeneid* bequeathed to the West a powerful foundation myth, but one centered more on the divine Homer, "the poet," as the wellspring of literature than on pallid, pious Aeneas as the father of Rome. Aeneas does finally get free of father Anchises, but Virgil's struggle with Homer continues to the end without even a forecast of victory.

Of Dante, E. M. W. Tillyard notes that it is not the occasional Ulysses or Farinata that makes the heroic impression, "it is rather the vast exercise of will that went to the shaping of the whole poem."[8] Dante proclaims his own—Christian— victory by bringing Virgil right into the fiction with him as a guide, then leaving him behind, lamented and absorbed. The form itself becomes autobiographical in explaining the act of literary derivation that gave it birth. Speaking in the vernacular, it is Roman Virgil himself who christens Italian as a literary language. Where novels have authors, writers of epic also proclaim themselves authored by the tradition, as Dante notes when he greets his ghostly guide as "lo mio maestro e 'l mio autore." What epic uniquely can offer for glory and reproach is the ability to array All That Precedes as a foil for the current dispensation, and to do so with the particular authority of a form that was itself in Athens, Rome, and Florence. Where the

historical novel, a patently modern form, must often accept the
anachronism of presenting old wine in new skins, epic offers a
tradition as old as the human events described, yet one incomparably quick at recapitulating millennia of culture by the merest
gesture. Devices like rosy dawns, adjectives suspended to mock
epithets ("Stately, plump . . ."), comparisons of a warrior to a
flame or a lion, or the image of a flickering bough draw the
knowledgeable reader into an underworld of fallen empires and
their unfading literatures.

Fully realized, then, epic may be said to have a double
plot: partly about heroes, partly about its own durability as a
form. From the advent of literacy to the current day, epics,
through their various levels of allusion, as well as through explicit
acknowledgment (for example, Joyce's choice of title for *Ulysses*),
have transmitted the fossilized strata of the epochs of literary
development that led up to themselves, that is, of artists' picking
up the work of other artists—a record that may contain a tale
larger than a given work's announced plot. For that plot will
concern at most the emergence of a single sense of nationhood
or creed, another Rome, while the embedded record of literary
genealogy traces the movement of culture from nation to nation,
language to language, religion to religion: *Iliad* to *Odyssey* to
Aeneid to *Divine Comedy*. This is not a list of separate items
in the way that novels are discrete from one another, but the
incremental record of a single pilgrimage to an eternally receding
shrine: to Ithaca, to Rome, to the City of God, or to a Moscow
or Dublin that is and is not all of these places.

Even in summoning the weight of antiquity, this tradition
favors newcomers. As Vico formulated, after decadence comes
a *ricorso*, another Homer in another heroic culture. The quest
myths that underlie the tradition allow movement forward in
time or space to become movement backward, so that the end
becomes the beginning, the last stands first, and innocence
constitutes authority. For both Aeneas and Moses, the long
exodus to a promised but unseen land proves to be a racial

homecoming. The newcomers to that land are its true and original lords. Christianity intensifies the paradox of the first and last, and of the child that shall lead them. The road to Gethsemane returns to and repairs the first garden, and the line of David ends where it began, now in an unfallen Adam. Similarly, Virgil could suggest Augustus not merely as the latest Roman strongman but as the renewal of his line, the new Aeneas. These myths of return have implications that make them central to their cultures. In combining the classical and Christian inheritances, the epic tradition enables a culture that perceives itself as somehow new, or that expresses itself in a yet unestablished literary language—as once Virgil's Rome, so later Dante's Florence and Gogol's Russia—to claim spiritual authority beyond its years by involving itself in the very origins of this migrating, self-regenerative culture that always flowers best on its latest frontier.

Starting late and in the east, the Russian renaissance followed the Roman pattern not less but more directly than had the former provinces of the Western empire. Just as the *Odyssey* translation of Livius Andronicus inaugurated Latin as a literary language, so an early reviewer, N. Polevoi, proclaimed Gnedich's *Iliad* (1801–29) to be "a treasurehouse of language...[that] exposes the richness, power, and resources of our own language."[9] We shall shortly encounter Gogol's comparable claims for Zhukovsky's *Odyssey*. Accommodating their resistant language to the Greek hexameter signified literary legitimacy for the Russians no less than for the Romans. For most of its history, the Roman West had known Greek, that both of Homer and of the New Testament, only as filtered through Latin. The Cyrillic alphabet puts the Russians in a different and closer tradition. Of the literary inheritance, a grammarian of the sixteenth or seventeenth century remarked that "Greek and Slavonic letters are like a lamb with its mother (for the Slavonic have proceeded from the Greek)—both of them resemble and harmonize with each other."[10] Lomonosov, for Pushkin the "Pe-

ter the Great of Russian literature," was typically heir to that
tradition. Educated in the Slavonic-Greek-Latin Academy in
Moscow, he translated parts of Homer (as well as of Virgil and
Ovid), proclaiming that "I consider the best of all poets to be
Homer."[11] As Philotheus's progression—Rome, Byzantium,
Moscow—indicates, literature, the empire, and the Church all
passed through a formative interlude in Italy, but the Byzantine-
Muscovite axis had its own unmediated proximity to Athens,
as to Jerusalem. Following in Vico's footsteps, German Ro-
manticism and the scholarship that followed on Wood and Wolf
located a bardic and folkloric Homer before and outside of the
European tradition, so that Tolstoy in "What Is Art?" could
place Homer next to the Bible as the last "good, supreme art"
still accessible to the masses.[12] There are independent strands
of epic inheritance from Homer to the Byzantine "Epic Cycle
of Digenis Akritas" and from there into the Kievan period of
Russian literature (through old-Russian translations).

To give themselves a language and a literature, the Russians
did have to free themselves from the dead weight of Byzantine
as well as of French influence. As in the West, it was the
classical grandparent that was called in to counteract the medieval parent. Homer worship was a sustained fashion in the
nineteenth century. Not only did Tolstoy place Homer next to
the Bible, but the youthful Dostoevsky likened him to Christ,[13]
just as Gogol had marked the serious turn in his career by
revising "Taras Bulba" to be more Homeric than Homer[14] and
in his final published letters treated the *Odyssey* almost like
holy writ in explaining the bases for patriarchal society.

Sunt lacrimae rerum: epic's excellent, if self-involved, memory also punctures the youthful dreams of national uniqueness
and unending mission. A third Rome implies a fourth. In fact,
it was the now much replaced Rome herself that invented the
migrating capital as a propagandistic device through her claim
to be the new Troy. Memory is not a natural ally of chauvinism.
In succeeding as the Homer of Rome, Virgil also incited gen-

erations of pretenders to become the Virgil of Florence, or Protestant England, or Portugal, or Russia; there will be others. By a final irony, it was in some measure the enduring vigor of Virgil's influence that inspired the Romantics to redirect their emulation to Homer. Epic's second plot, its embedded genealogy, brings arguments more powerful than any creed or nationalism or individual career that it briefly serves. The official pieties about grand results rest uneasily on the tradition's accumulating and ineradicable documentation of fallen empires and vain human wishes. In conjuring up dead glories, the latter-day bard may even find that they are not quite dead enough. No later capital outshines fallen Troy.

In the central tradition that stretches from Homer to Milton, as to Tolstoy, Joyce, and doubtless beyond, it is less literary similarity that links the texts than their memories of one another in a transmission that has moved from song to written poetry to prose and sometimes back again and that, on the crucial topic of heroic engagement, oscillates unendingly between solemnity and mockery. "Memory," noted Walter Benjamin fifty years ago, "is the epic faculty par excellence,"[15] alone responsible for producing the transmission through successive generations. To compare epic and novel is not necessarily to differentiate literary kinds but to contrast the novel as a category (unbounded and indeterminate as it may be) with a tradition, the epic, that can easily flow into and out of this corpus as it has others. We might more accurately speak of epic as a cycle than as a genre, that is, as texts associated less by likeness than by a continuing thread of narrative and allusive gestures (for instance, Dante's Virgil-guide, Milton's proemia) that announce each new text as the final chapter of what precedes. There are, to be sure, continuing characteristics: a strong protagonist, breadth of canvas, some sort of divine apparatus.[16] As has been repeatedly proven, these characteristics are notoriously poor predictors of where the cycle will next turn. Crafty Odysseus is profoundly not where the *Iliad* was heading, and, detached from the in-

evitability of hindsight, Aeneas and Dante-pilgrim mark similarly odd jumps. The legions of poets who have rewritten the
Aeneid are mostly forgotten; it was much more likely the subversive Ovid's parody of the epic project in fifteen metamorphic
books of universal history that enabled Dante and Milton to
reconstitute the Virgilian voice. Goethe's abandoned *Achilleid*
captures less of Homer than does *Hermann and Dorothea*.
Though the tradition advances by such dodges and displace-
ments, in each new chapter the structure of allusion leaves no
doubt about where it has been.

The bid for inclusion within this cycle involves claims to
literary legitimacy and cultural centrality of most interest to
literatures on the periphery. After an initial dialogue with heroic
literature (Cervantes, Rabelais, Fielding, Sterne), the European
novel ceased to be preoccupied with this inheritance, so that
the double plot mostly drops out of sight. Within the English
novel, Tillyard's "epic strain," Leavis's "great tradition," and
Kermode's notion of "the classic" trace other forms of magnitude
and ambition.[17] Manzoni's treatise on the historical novel charts
how in Italy the cumulative weight of the tradition from Virgil
to Tasso became too much to bear; after Tasso, "the public
wanted to call the writing of such poems to a halt."[18] Yet again
it is on the frontier, in colonial literatures, that the cycle re-
emerges. Diagnosing the death of epic in Europe, Hegel in his
Aesthetics declared that the aspiring writer of epic "will be
necessarily restricted to the portrayal of the victory of some
future and intensely vital rationality of the American nation
over the prison-house of the spirit which for ever pursues its
monotonous task of self-adjustment and particularization."[19]
Other cases in the West parallel the Russian claim to some such
election. Attempting the great Irish novel in the conquerors'
language, Joyce called in the epic grandparent, Homer, to cut
the Englishmen's tradition down to scale, as did Melville in
Moby Dick, his "prose Epic on whaling,"[20] a work emphatically
other than the bourgeois English novel. As telling in its failed

ambitions is Joel Barlow's *Columbiad* (1807), which deployed
Homer, Virgil, and Noah Webster's simplified American spell-
ings to break the ties with England.

The "heroic age" itself thrives best at the borders, as we
see in the tendency of the last two centuries to transfer the term
epic to oral traditions. For a period the invented bard Ossian
stood as Homer's truest successor. Even in evolved literatures,
bards do well to claim barbarian blood: to Irish eyes, the Celtic
inheritance puts Dublin closer to Ithaca than is London and
empowers Yeats to dream of Byzantium. As doomed companion,
Queequeg makes a better descendent of Patroclus than could
anyone who had heard of Patroclus, and it was the still un-
mastered wildness of Americans themselves that enabled Melville to construct the Iliadic tale of wrath, Ahab's as once
Achilles', in conjunction with the biblical quest of Leviathan,
now become a white whale.

In its origins and evolution, the word *epic* has far more to
do with the questions of formation of tradition that we are
raising than with matters of form or style. For the Greeks, *epos*
was an utterance—a word, a speech, a poem. In reference to
verse it designated the vast body of poems in dactylic hexameter,
not just the *Iliad* and *Odyssey* but other heroic poems in long
and short forms, as well as hymns, some comic verse (the
Margites), and didactic poems (Hesiod).[21] It is prestige that
attaches *epos* more specifically to Homer, since for the Greeks
Homer was simply "the poet," as Shakespeare is to us "the
bard." The use of *epic* for the center and pinnacle is more basic
than whatever texts are promoted to that position at one time
or another. The term is closer in use to *classic*, a perspective
or sense of literary topography describing a corpus with a center,
than it is to *lyric* or *drama* as they refer to original modes of
performance, or even to the radically indeterminate category of
the novel, a countering perspective where, though various centers and priorities can be argued (classics, a "great tradition"),
the term is applied with no sense of such election and is con-

stantly being redefined by what is produced. Unlike other things that might be called genres (or forms, kinds, species, modes), epic tends to be self-limiting—that is, restricted to its successes. The also-rans may still receive the term from their editors but do not come to mind when the "epic tradition" is being discussed. In naming an "American epic," most respondents would find prose (*Moby Dick*) less of a disqualification than failure (*The Columbiad*).[22]

The other identifying characteristic of epic is that it is long dead, indeed recurrently dead. In our era it is the novel that has killed it, just as in earlier times it was done in by philosophy (so declared Plato, extruding Homer from the Republic), by tragedy (in Aristotle's diagnosis in the *Poetics*), by confessional literature (so Augustine, turning from Dido in his *Confessions*), and then by romance (for example, Ariosto—but perhaps this was the same death that epic had died with Apollonius Rhodius almost two millennia before[23] or in the somewhat later Greek romances). Even in ages when it is not being written or perhaps read with much enthusiasm, epic maintains its preeminence as the victim of choice for the currently dominant literary form. As we shall soon discuss, it is as the victim of the novel that Lukács and Bakhtin present the epic to us. Bakhtin further argues that the novel is literature's ultimate because ultimately indeterminate form, that is, the infinitely flexible genre that precludes the emergence of any new genres.

Before turning to these theorists we might note the signs that epic may survive this latest death better than the novel will outlast its permanent victory.[24] Long before Eisenstein used Milton's War in Heaven as the shooting script for the battle on the ice in *Alexander Nevsky* (1938),[25] film had singled out epic as its predecessor and esteemed victim much more than it had the novel, though in practice it is the act of novel-reading that film-going replaces. For all the novels that are turned into screenplays, "epic" has currency as a mode of cinema in a way that "novelistic" does not.

The various cinematic applications of "epic" provide a telling reflection of the complexity of its literary uses. "Screen epic" is a thriving branch of popular culture that has inherited certain stereotypical qualities of literary epic: scale, celebration of nationhood (*Birth of a Nation, Napoleon*) or creed (*Ben-Hur, The Ten Commandments*), and evocation of a past so closed and distant that its iconography translates easily into the future of science fiction (*Star Wars*).[26] At its best, especially in the tradition that stretches from Griffith to Kurosawa, this archaizing form maintains its currency remarkably well, especially in comparison to the rapid obsolescence of much literary experiment (the theater of the absurd, the *nouveau roman*).

Working from Brecht's concept of "epic theater," film theory uses the word quite differently to describe a self-conscious cinema unconstrained by those unities of time, place, and action that Aristotelians stipulated for tragedy. Inspired especially by screen clowns like Charlie Chaplin and Buster Keaton, Brecht saw the externality of film, its capacity for discontinuity, plotlessness, and stylization of gesture as a tool against the bourgeois mentality of the novel.[27] The audiences "alienated" and provoked to ideological reflection by such films, most notably those of Godard, are taken to be at a polar remove from the escapists lulled by the "screen epics." Whereas those costume dramas aspire without embarrassment to the prestige of monumental art, this other and didactic mode of "epic" cinema can instead provide a critique of tradition itself, as in the famous case of Godard's *Le Mépris* (1963), a film about a filming of the *Odyssey* by a Brecht-quoting director, "Fritz Lang" (played by Fritz Lang), bullied by a crass, capitalist American producer (Jack Palance).[28] In his allegory of the "shipwreck of modernity," as Godard called it, "the eye of the camera watching these characters in search of Homer replaces that of the gods watching over Ulysses and his companions."[29]

These are but straws in the wind, though sufficient to warrant caution in diagnosing the death of cultural forms. Epic is still alive enough as a generative principle to be called in by Brecht as an antidote (and successor) to capitalist art forms and to inspire Godard's apotheosis of the camera. Differently understood, it also lives on in the popular imaginaton to organize production and consumption of a certain kind of commercial film spectacle. Those disparate applications of the term reflect the dialectic of the epic tradition as it has always advanced both by the big canvasses (whether of popular or high art) and by the critiques and dismantlings of them (in other words, as much by mock-epic as by achieved national epics).[30] The development of the cinema has replicated the age-old literary quandary about whether "epic" denotes the largest sweep of action and of meaning—the aspiration to totality—or the most retentive mode of artistic self-consciousness. The evolution of serious film has not been toward the anarchic and ahistorical proliferation once expected but toward the assertion of archetypes, the codification of allusion, the induction of its makers into a guild of *auteurs* celebrating their forebears. Once the streets of Los Angeles or São Paulo or Melbourne can be shot and edited as a recapitulation of the Berlin of the thirties, the Rome of the fifties, or the utopian Los Angeles of the studios, cinema acquires its own double plot: the quick, capacious memory, the latent internationalism that we have associated with epic. A rhetoric of jump cuts, voice-overs, and tracking shots serves this end neither better nor worse than do similes and epithets. Celluloid classicism works increasingly from a pantheon of Eisenstein, Griffith, Lang, Hitchcock, Godard, Truffaut. Yet, as in the literary tradition, such reflexivity does not necessarily disrupt emotional engagement and the suspension of disbelief, but in providing imaginative distance and protective irony can allow heroic fantasies new scope.

Having survived the advent of writing and then of printing, epic as a process of tradition forming and cultural centering is more resilient than purely written forms like the novel or short story, though it must survive each transition by a kind of "grandfather clause," a bemused toleration of it as a living anachronism. Current prospects suggest that it is much more likely the novel itself will end in the graveyard of epic's other destroyers than that epic will forego the millennial parasitism whereby it thrives through the nostalgia and condescension of its various replacements until they are themselves replaced. Yet when literary theorists call epic dead, they do so at the invitation of its practitioners, who know how to exploit this nostalgia. For two and a half millennia, epic has been a song sung at its own funeral, always deepening its poignancy with the promise that any revival of it is the last, the very last, that we are to hear. The epic cycle is a book composed entirely of final chapters.

The Death of Epic

Too big to be overlooked and firmly planted at the cultural center, epics thus elude literary historians by presenting their credentials so duplicitously. From epoch to epoch the form comes unexpectedly alive only to find another consummation and die yet another final death. As such, the epic is a convenient starting point for teleological theorists, from Aristotle to Bakhtin, who need something big, simple, and defunct as a basis of comparison.[31] It is instructive to review the fate of Aristotle's dictum that tragedy had absorbed and superseded epic, for within a century after he wrote this, tragedy was reabsorbed into the main epic tradition: Medea moved from Euripides' stage to the hexameters of Apollonius Rhodius's *Argonautica* and then, after being dramatized in the interval by Ennius, lived on in Virgil's Dido. Epic would die another death, this time for doctrinal reasons, when that erstwhile intemperate admirer of Dido, Augustine of Hippo, turned from Virgil and the pagans to scripture and the new form of the confession. Yet the full literary realization of such autobiography, Dante's *Divina Commedia*, would bring Virgil and epic back from the grave. To be sure, Dante, like Augustine, was still marching past the tribe of Dido, now led by Francesca da Rimini, but Virgil the seducer (for Augustine) had become Virgil the guide, who could be left behind atop Mount Purgatory, not because his form was moribund, but because it was now securely reborn and redeemed.

This second death proved to be only the start of Virgil's modern *Nachleben*, for he was destined to be conjured time and again by allusion so that he might confess his obsolescence and once more bequeath his authority. As was noted above, such ghosts favor the frontiers and, within such emergent cultures, outcasts. In their various forms of exile and disenfranchisement, Dante, Milton, Joyce, and Pasternak all provide terms to understand what will be our central case, Gogol's removal to Rome. To this may be added a salient American example, where, as with Gogol, sexual identity plays a central role. To establish Nebraska as a literary landscape within the European canon, Willa Cather in *My Ántonia* has the classicist Gaston Cleric and his pupil, Jim Burden, self-consciously re-enact the Virgil-Dante relationship even as they read Virgil's *Georgics*, which introduced the Italian landscape into the same tradition. In *The Professor's House*, Tom Outland, like Burden an orphan, reads the *Aeneid* amid the ruins of Blue Mesa (a version of Mesa Verde) and imagines before him the very towers of Troy.[32] It is outsiders—Dante in his terrifying valley, Milton in his dark study, Outland on his lonely bluff, and Cather as heir to a European and male guild—who are most apt to see ghosts, as we shall find with Gogol and his dead souls.

For writers continuing the cycle, the "death of epic" is a topos.[33] When Virgil said early in his career that he would sing no "kings and battles," he may have meant it (*Eclogue* 6.3–5), since Homeric epic was for his generation unattainable and perhaps undesired. Whatever pressures of political circumstance (Augustus) and ambition intervened, he did go on to write other things, so that his statement now stands in his oeuvre as a prelude to epic. The epic pilgrimage to which Virgil was giving permanent definition thus starts with refusal, then surmounts it. Within the same tradition Dante-pilgrim similarly declines the invitation to join *la bella scuola* of Homer, Horace, Ovid, and Lucan. They stand with dignity as a closed chapter that we might call "the death of epic." Dante could join them only by foregoing the voyage to Beatrice. Yet he can arrive at Beatrice only with the help of refugees from that *scuola*, Virgil and Statius, who equally suggest the chapter as not closed or closable. A heresy larger than joining the pagan bards on their own terms would be to conclude that their art, or any art, is not capable of transfiguration.

The nearly obligatory *ecphrases* that descend from Achilles' shield in *Iliad* 18 provide a demonstration of how the cycle fails of closure. Entering Carthage in *Aeneid* 1, Aeneas sees on the temple of Juno reliefs of the Trojan War and, observing the sufferings of himself and his people thus memorialized by Dido, is heartened and seduced. Like the Sirens' song, this account of "kings and battles" can lure the unguarded audience to oblivion. By staying with Dido and marrying that glorious past, Aeneas, like Dante with the bards of *Inferno* 4, would go no farther. Yet those very bas-reliefs, Virgil's symbol of a defunct and entrapping art, are the literary stuff out of which Dante crafts the redemptive cycle divinely carved on the first ledge of the mountain (Mary, David, and Trajan in *Purgatory* 10). The very rocks have risen. Epic is dead, long live epic.

On the death of literary forms, Alastair Fowler proposes the following rule of thumb: "Pronounce a genre dead if works related to it directly are no longer widely read, so that its forms have become unintelligible without scholarly effort."[34] On this score, Homeric epic remains more alive for the modern reader than many of its successors, like the Greek romances or Menippean satire. Unlike the novel, the epic lives not just because it is written and bought but also because it is taught and incorporated into central belief systems. The contrast of epic and novel misleads because only a three-way comparison—novel, epic, and scripture—begins to lead to clarity. To note that the

novel comes from the Christian era as the epic does from the
pagan nearly reverses their actual literary life in the nineteenth
century. For the novel, especially in Russian eyes, was a secular
and Western form, while the epic, even Homer and Virgil by
posthumous conversion, had a status in Christian letters and
ecclesiastical education older than Russia itself.[35] The prospect
that the epic might be a dead tradition might have been less
worrisome than the fact that the novel, for all its current aesthetic
possibilities, had been spiritually stillborn. The sense of historical time moving to apocalypse, a place where the European
novel could never go, was not outmoded for Gogol, nor is it,
for that matter, for Solzhenitsyn. For such pilgrims, the novel
is only a way station. To call a novel *The First Circle* suggests
that a form beyond the novel impends.

Since the novel is the later and currently generative form,
some theorists, like Lukács[36] and Bakhtin[37] have sought to define
it by emphasizing its amorphousness, vitality, and open-endedness in contradistinction to the closed chapter that epic supposedly represents. Both assume that once material has flowed
down to the novel and to the swamps of post-Enlightenment
consciousness from the Pierian spring of epic, it never flows
back uphill. Both theorists take epic (almost exclusively Homer)
and novel as epitomes of their respective ages.[38] What sets the
forms and ages apart is the onset of indeterminacy in spiritual
as in political life, in literary form as in language. For Lukács
the characteristic of the epic age, and above all Homer, is "the
adequacy of the deeds to the soul's inner demand for greatness,
for unfolding, for wholeness. . . . Being and destiny, adventure
and accomplishment, life and essence are then identical concepts."[39] Yet the stable, fulfilling age thus described is not a
heroic age so much as a patriarchal and hierarchical one, whereas
the *Iliad* at least is more insistently antiauthoritarian. Lukács's
description fits the well-meaning Hector far more than it does
Achilles. Consider the arc of Achilles' journey to "fulfillment":
his murderous wrath against Agamemnon is turned against the

whole Achaean army, which is saved only when he finally turns it against Hector and himself. What modern readers tend to find compelling in the conclusion is the remarkable scene where Achilles and Priam, momentarily but with profound understanding, step outside destinies that they both regret. Lukács's hazy ideal scarcely surprises, of course, since it was only under some such protective mist that pagan epic could be allowed to enter Christian classrooms.

In fact, the heroes of classical epic, though not necessarily the secondary characters, tend to embody just those characteristics that both theorists see as setting the novel apart from the epic. The "spiritual homelessness," the ruptured linkage of code to feeling that Lukács sees as the death knell of the heroic age is in fact what sets Achilles apart from his peers,[40] as it does Aeneas and Dante-pilgrim from theirs. Indeed, such spiritual crises may have been the integrating theme that allowed shorter lays to be organized into the larger structures of Homeric epic. The *Iliad* strings together various duels and days of glory (for Diomedes, Agamemnon, Hector, Patroclus) that enact heroic values straightforwardly enough and would seem to represent the earlier tradition. Yet the larger tale in which these elements are embedded, the wrath and revenge of Achilles, pivots on questioning, rejecting, and in some measure finally ignoring the very code that he supremely embodies.[41] It is the critique of war that enables the poem to become the great tale of war.

Similarly, the new scale allows the traditional trickster of folklore not just to overcome witches and ogres along the way, as Odysseus does Circe and the Cyclops, but to rejoin a whole family turned deceivers (Penelope and Telemachus), so that the intricate process of recognizing one another goes beyond the magic tokens and dropped masks of trickster tales to become a complex analysis of the epistemology of memory and desire. Odysseus, famous now and battered, finds himself in competition with the image of the beloved king and father who had left home twenty years before. The requisite happy ending,

stable and complete, of an "epic age" is attained in Ithaca only
when the notion of happiness itself has been permanently de-
stabilized by the new subjectivities discovered in memory,
dreams, and deceit in a text that is itself a self-conscious response
to the *Iliad*.[42] In Homer, the glorious past does, as Lukács
observes, maintain its absolute superiority over the present; but
it is a glory that instructively dismantles, discredits, and ana-
lyzes itself. If the "epic age" is prephilosophical and unreflective,
the great epics are its most philosophical and least characteristic
part.

Lukács justly observes that between antiquity and the modern era (as epitomized by the epic and the novel) stands a vast
increase in literary attention to alienation and spiritual homelessness. He describes thereby one of the attractions of the epic
tradition for novelists who want to overcome the indeterminacy
of the novel, the anomie of their age, or their own marginality
or that of their culture. Epic does—if only in the retrospect that
makes it seem fixed, confident, and official—promise focus and
structure. Yet when these great works are executed, tendencies
emerge for the wrong hero to carry the tale, for the oldest and
doctrinally least acceptable stratum of material to seem the
freshest and most appealing, often the pagan rather than the
Christian. This most traditional of forms may celebrate some
new dispensation in its overt plot but make quite a different
argument in the internationalism and ungovernable self-regen-
eration of the allusive style, that second plot of epic which does
not respect shifts of doctrine or politics or fashion. It was Dante's
intention to move his readers beyond his lively, pagan Inferno,
as it was Milton's to get them past the antique heroics of Satan.
Not all readers stay the course.

In this early work on epic and novel, Lukács is following
in the tradition of Goethe, Schiller, and most immediately Hegel
by romanticizing Homer's era and reasserting the ancient habit
of leading universal history from some golden age. Lukács
harbors hopes of revolutionary change in bourgeois culture that

will restore such an epoch, and the epic that expresses it. Though such nostalgia has more sources than can here be disentangled, it is clear that for the theorist this lost paradise provides a manageable basis of comparison for the complexities to follow. Moreover, even Romantics and socialists could not quickly cut lose from pagan literature's long cohabitation with scripture and its notion of innocent and fallen ages. Thanks to the curriculum, epic is wedded to the youth of the reader as to the youth of the race, a process that Joyce depicts in Stephen Dedalus's classroom in the second chapter of *Ulysses*. Lukács was not yet thirty years old when he wrote his celebration of Homer. As Macaulay in 1825 observed of the names in Milton's catalogues:

> Like the dwelling-place of our infancy revisited in
> manhood, like the song of our country heard in a
> strange land, they produce upon us an effect wholly
> independent of their intrinsic value. One transports us
> back to a remote period of history. Another places us
> among the novel scenes and manners of a distant region.
> A third evokes all the dear classical recollections of
> childhood, the schoolroom, the dog-eared Virgil, the
> holiday, and the prize.[43]

These habits affect writers of epics and the audiences for which they see themselves as writing, even as they affect theorists. Even if there had been no "epic age," the assumption that there was one shapes the tradition and glamorizes epic ambitions, as they mix cultural imperialism and a quest for lost innocence.

Perfidious and uncontrollable as it may prove to those who try to master it, epic has a tendency to become fixed and monolithic when viewed over the shoulder. Its definitive heroes are volatile, treacherous, or neurotic (Achilles, Odysseus, Aeneas); from afar, they are often mistaken for patriarchs, much as Apollo and Dionysus snatched from context have been made to serve iconographically for Christ. Inscribed in the canon, translated, and taught in school, its great successes seem sedate.

Indeed, they do lose something in the original: certainty. The "realms of gold" that Keats found in Chapman's Homer may have seemed a splendid monstrosity to a Greek audience used to short heroic lays. As Kirk observes of the monumental poem, "by the normal canons of heroic song this kind of poem is an aberration."[44] Some singer, either heroically ambitious or assisted by the new technology of writing, was stringing together a week's entertainment from Trojan tales, borrowings from other cycles, catalogues, riotous *Götterkomödie*, self-parody (Thersites, Nestor), *ecphrasis*, and a hero, given to tantrums and existential speculation, who actually fights for only four books out of twenty-four. Legions of textual surgeons have not belabored the "Homeric question" for two centuries to cure an excess of uniformity. Virgil wrote by the thousands a neoteric verse form developed to be read by the dozens and, through this massive miniature, refracted his encomium of Rome into myriad congruent and dissonant voices, not so much sung as quoted, overheard, dreamt, meant, and not meant. Beneath the stately and unified diction are a welter of generic influences: Homeric, Alexandrian, and Roman epos; Greek and Roman tragedy and lyric; oratory and decrees. Dante mixed satire, pagan heroics, scripture, lyric, Ovidian metamorphoses, and homilies as he circumnavigated the cosmos in the vernacular and wrote universal history as autobiography. Had they not come to define the tradition, these experiments might rank as travesties.

Polyphony and Pentecost

Mikhail Bakhtin centers his analysis not on genres but on the opposed generative principles of all literature, the "epic" and the "novelistic." The now defunct "epic" derives from a monoglot culture (Bakhtin cites only Homeric Greece) that can express its central values in a "high and straightforward" word without the interplay of voices, ironies, and languages of the "novelistic" as it emerges from periods of linguistic mixture and confrontation. The "novelistic" consolidates itself in the orientalizing ("Hellenistic") mode of Greek culture (after Alexander, third century B.C.E. onward) and in bilingual Rome, then reasserts itself strongly in the linguistic struggle that brought the vernaculars out of Latin in the Renaissance. Interestingly, the polyphonic forms that Bakhtin sees as the telos of literary development are those satiric, personalistic, many-voiced texts that Gogol a century before had described, in his survey of poetry from Lomonosov to Pushkin and Zhukovsky, as being distinctively Russian. The penultimate chapter of his final work, *Selected Passages from Correspondence with Friends*, entitled "On the Essence of Russian Poetry and on Its Originality," locates quintessential Russianness in polyglossia, the power of language as it is only now being discovered by the Russians themselves:

> After all, our extraordinary language is itself a secret. In it are all the tones and all the shades, all the transitional sounds from the solidest to the tenderest and softest; it is unlimited and can, living like life, at every moment be constantly enriched, drawing, on the one hand, from the sublime words of the biblical language of the Church, and, on the other, choosing to select accurate terms from the innumerable dialects scattered through our provinces, thus having the possibility in one and the same speech of ascending to heights inaccessible to any other language and of being lowered to a level of simplicity appreciatively felt by the dullest of men. . . . [45]

Gogol's history organizes itself around an absence: Russian literature does not have at its center a work to pull the pieces together. "It [poetry] has accumulated only in one pile innumerable little hints of our diverse qualities; it has brought together in one depository various unconnected sides of our many-sided nature" (p. 243). The problem for the Russians strikingly parallels the bilingualism that Bakhtin finds generative for the Romans, the incorporation of a more evolved literary language (French, like Greek) that forces the new literature to proceed with particularly acute self-consciousness—to speak, as it were, always in the mode of quotation.

Gogol is a particularly interesting source because he initiates an epic project that is inimical to Bakhtin's values. His attempt to move the novel toward being authoritative, culturally central, and nationalistic, as in some measure Gogol does, is to Bakhtin a betrayal of what is lively, subversive, and anti-authoritarian in the "novelistic." Bakhtin considers *War and Peace* monophonic and claims that Gogol "lost Russia" in trying to work the "novelistic" beginning of *Dead Souls* toward some kind of monumentality.

"Epic" as defined by Bakhtin may prove to be a phenomenon of reception more than a generative principle. As Morson has shown, as a narrative *War and Peace* responds fruitfully to Bakhtin's theory.[46] Yet the book has another life, for when it is taught in translation with classroom materials that gloss over its pointed anomalies, this once aberrant and provocative unmaking of the novel stands as an unproblematic and definitive "classic." The now canonical epics themselves came from the very moments of linguistic "interanimation" that Bakhtin emphasizes. Greek lurks behind the Latin of Virgil and Ovid, as does Latin behind Milton's English and Dante's Italian. When Gogol himself, in his retreat to Rome to write the great Russian novel, used Italian to liberate Russian from French, his gesture seemed as much a part of the Virgilian-Dantesque tradition as of "novelistic" tendency. All such works are received as monophonic and authoritarian once they have been flattened by translation, removed from the controversies of their time, and imposed on the young. Even Bakhtin's beloved Rabelais and Dostoevsky experience that dull fate when they become required reading as classics—that is, in Bakhtin's terms, as "epics."

Bakhtin's field theory of literary production so powerfully discredits the pieties and simplifications of literary historians, those purveyors of category and period, that it thwarts even his own attempt to locate "epic" and "novelistic" as historical principles. He skirts the historical paradox of how "novelistic" are the processes by which the cultural center gets constituted in the first place. To take a turning point that is paradoxical in all such histories, his Socrates midwifes "dialogism" as Plato's does philosophy. Yet a contradiction lurks between these claims: Plato's dialogues may be the prototype of "novelistic" style, as well as of free inquiry, but they scarcely serve the spirit of carnival. To be sure, Kristeva sees Bakhtin's analysis as a corrective to Nietzsche's attack on Socrates as a destroyer of some such tendency (that is, the Dionysian as it anticipates Bakhtin's "carnivalesque").[47] Yet, in the larger historical perspective, Nietzsche's critique retains its power. The primordial spirit of Dionysus (or of carnival) has no enemies more potent than the Academy, the transcendencies of Platonism, and, ultimately, Christian theology.

We are left with an ineradicable paradox: the basic pattern of Bakhtin's larger history is contained and reversed already in the distance traversed between Socrates in the marketplace, affirming nothing but the value of questioning, and Plato, who passed down his esoteric doctrines, the absolutes of Platonism, behind the walls of the Academy. A public gadfly inspired the foundation of the Ivory Tower; free inquiry hardened into a party line; the "popular" prose form of the dialogue supported intellectual, political, and, eventually, theological elitism. In a word, the polyphonic gave birth to the monophonic. Part of the codification that simultaneously killed and immortalized Socrates' liberating assault on received wisdom and social convention was Plato's "novelistic" gift (and he has few rivals in prose) of capturing on paper the polyphony of Socrates as he is reported in action.

Bakhtin observes, "Neither an epic nor a tragic hero could ever step out in his own character during a pause in the plot or during an intermission: he has no face for it, no gesture, no language."[48] In contrast, Socrates presides over a world that has

no conventional plot, only intermissions. Here the great players
in history, like the *Symposium*'s drunken Alcibiades before the
Sicilian expedition, come stumbling in with their masks a-kilter,
and the gap between self and society becomes the beginning of
wisdom. Yet in making Socrates' life the new plot, the only true
plot, Plato created a world incomparably more seamless and
uniform, more ranked, centered, and organized than Homer's.
Achilles only *exemplified* the old heroism (and that but fitfully);
Socrates was coextensive with the new, the flesh made spirit.
Plato's playful, richly voiced prose promoted the very cultural
monolith that the "novelistic" dismantles.

Bakhtin's stylistic analyses of seriocomic forms in antiquity
remain unsurpassed, but ideologically he nods, and recent scholarship leaves little to support the history that he implies. Popular
laughter, daily life, and the open-ended present come into literature with Aristophanes' comedies, as they do in Plato's dialogues, and Aristophanes leaves no doubts: Socrates is no friend
of the *dēmos*. The comedian does not restrict his characters or
his audience to an elite, but Old Comedy is something of a
literary dead end. As in the Platonic dialogues, popular laughter
is destined to be memorialized mostly in libraries. Another of
Bakhtin's central examples, Petronius also promotes popular
forms into artistic prose but, as a courtier of Nero, is presumably
not expressing the *Volksgeist* in any simple way. Scholarship
since Bakhtin has undermined the impression that the descent
of literature into the streets and into the open-ended present
might reflect movements of authorship or readership. Apart
from the mostly lost farces, the emergent popular forms that
Bakhtin favors tend to be regarded now as "probably written
as lighter reading for the intelligentsia," as Bowie observes of
Lucan and the Greek novelists.[49] It was the earlier forms like
Homeric epic and Attic tragedy, which Bakhtin sees as stifling
the popular imagination, that in fact entertained and unified
the whole society.

As other cornerstones of Europe as the Culture of the Book, Homer and the Bible are equally involved in the paradoxes of the oral passing into the written, in this case the process of folklore becoming textually fixed and scriptural.[50] Much of Bakhtin's project can be seen as tracing the recovery in prose of the "voice" lost as oral forms reduced themselves to the silent page. Just as between Socratic play and Platonic doctrine, we are forced to make other distinctions: between epic as sung and created and Bakhtin's "epic" as received; between the Bible as created and scripture as imposed. Both the Homeric epics and the Hebrew Bible are aggregates of radically heterogeneous material that does not become less complex by being compiled. Even in the *Iliad* philologists have come to appreciate a quality of multivoicedness in the tension of speeches and narrative.[51]

Palestine and the Greek coast of Asia, Homer's Ionia, are Bakhtin's linguistic crossroads par excellence.[52] It seems misleading to treat either aggregate, Bible or Homer, as the dead cultural center and the outgrowth of some organized political intention when the "national" identities being asserted are more caused than celebrated by the texts themselves. In antiquity, both Greece (never a nation) and Israel have a firmer identity in these texts than they did on the map. The texts' affirmation of hierarchy often involves irony: what are we to make of the king or patriarch as trickster (Odysseus, Jacob)? The cultural reach and narrative power that render this writ holy are oral, folkloric, quintessentially polyphonic. For Bible, as for epic, the lack of "interiority" is not a safe assumption.[53] It is the processes of reception—the reduction of performances to inviolable texts, of a lively industry to a few official survivors, and of a colorful *Kunstsprache* to flat, pious translationese—that create the impression of simplicity.[54] The monophony of "epic" may result more from our tone-deafness than from the processes that create the aggregations which then become the anchors of society.

Problematic as is Bakhtin's category of "epic" in historical terms, it does describe a phenomenon central to the traditions

we are tracing. For the poets themselves exploit the "epic" sense
of authority and centrality by parading their own grand inheritance and celebrating the canon they wish to join. Yet in the
very act of pretending that their inheritance is grand and fixed,
they distort it freely, as they must, and render the canon malleable. As was discussed above, the statuesque assemblage of
Virgil, Homer, Horace, Ovid, and Lucan in *Inferno* 4 gives only
a first and dangerous illusion of the canon, for Virgil's mobility
and the encounter with the converted Statius will redeem the
very concept of canon from its secular and ancient terms. Harold
Bloom finds a similar freedom in Milton's adaptation of epic
ecphrasis. Whereas Homer and Virgil miniaturized the world
on their heroes' shields, Milton presents Satan's shield as a
microcosm of his own literary antecedents, optically distorted
(complete with Galileo's glass) to fill his own needs: "Milton
does what Bacon hoped to do; Milton and Galileo become
ancients, and Homer, Virgil, Ovid, Dante, Tasso, Spencer become belated moderns."[55] At key moments in the epic pilgrimage, the tradition itself steps forward to guide the seeker. Yet
the tradition thus embodied may represent a reconceiving of
history more radical than Bakhtin's. In the name of theory he
may present an improbably one-dimensional Homer, but consider what Dante does to Virgil out of love: Virgilio speaks
Italian, after all, and recants part of the Latin verse of Roman
Virgil (*Inferno* 20). He turns out not only to have inspired
Statius but to have converted him to Christianity.[56] The cultural
center that epics celebrate keeps shifting, as does the frontier
from which they address that center.

If we separate epics as they came to be written from the
concept of monophonic "epic," which we are arguing to be
largely a result of reception, we find that Bakhtin's use of
counter-genre proves useful for describing the dialectic by which
the tradition advances. He notes that epics generate parodies
and reactions to themselves that then belong to another and
"novelistic" form. Our view is that these shorter forms—mock-

heroic, pastoral, and didactic poetry—regularly become reabsorbed into the larger syntheses that we are calling epic, which
grow all the more "novelistic" thereby. The *Iliad* and *Odyssey*
incorporate and derive from shorter forms at various levels of
seriousness (for example, the *Odyssey*'s Demodocus sings a
ribald tale of Aphrodite and Ares at 8.265–366). And archaic
epos presents a range of didactic verse (Hesiod), as well as the
Homeric Hymns' mixture of humor, etiology, and piety. Between
Homer and Virgil lie the countermonumental short, variegated
forms of the Alexandrians (Theocritus, Callimachus, Apollonius
Rhodius) that are reabsorbed into the larger forms of Virgil and
Ovid. Between Virgil and Dante one of the major links is the
counter-epic of the insouciant Ovid.[57] Within this familiar cycle
of serious monuments and the reactions thereto, even the most
unlikely swings are now well studied, for instance, that between
Ovid and the unsmiling Milton.[58] That successful epics temporarily exhaust the form was a commonplace assumption already in antiquity, and how a great cultural synthesis like the
Aeneid should leave Ovid to look elsewhere as he constructed
his fifteen books of universal history in ironic and metamorphic
terms needs no further explanation.

These ironic forms are not just a medium for epic concerns
to reformulate themselves between monumental syntheses—the
valleys between the peaks, as it were—but are often the mode
in which an opening can be made by epics or by novels in the
epic tradition. Though mock heroic was the path taken by Sterne
and Fielding to work forward from epic poetry to the novel,
Joyce was scarcely the first to demonstrate that the same path
also leads backward; we shall be arguing that case for Gogol.[59]
The larger epic journey, as mapped by Dante and then Milton,
begins infernally: with descent, mockery, and derision—that is,
with the central mock-heroic operations of seeing the great ones
of this world frozen, shrunk, and humiliated. Even the *Iliad*
begins, not with battle, but with heroes throwing tantrums.
Heroism manifests itself faster and more interestingly by its

deformations than by its triumphs, which, narratively, must always be rare and climactic. Indeed, it has never been supposedly useful, dignified triumph that fixes the paramount heroes in the mind but, rather, peculiar scenes like Achilles' mutilation of Hector's corpse, Odysseus' being beaten as a beggar, Heracles' killing of his wife and sons. The normative hero being normatively heroic can radiate glory from a temple frieze or metope but plays no more than a supporting role in epic (see Homer's Diomedes, Ajax, Patroclus, Sarpedon): there is just no story in it. The heroism that is the simple, static, ancient thing from which literary theory traces all the interesting variations and debunkings turns out to be more like the severe and focused idealism of classical sculpture, which Hegel and Nietzsche found a more manageable inspiration than the disruptive heroes of Greek poetry. In epic, a heroic figure can include all manner of contradictions—indeed must include them—as long as they are explosive contradictions. It is scarcely out of the question for Gogol in *Dead Souls* to start with infernal descent and conceive that it might be leading somewhere higher.

The serious shorter forms also figure in the epic tradition, indeed shape the canonical epic career as, following Virgil's pattern, it progressed from pastorals (the *stylus humilis*) to georgics (the *stylus mediocris*) and finally to the *Aeneid* (the *stylus gravis*)—a course followed in various ways by Dante, Ariosto, Milton, and Pope. We noted above that epic, though by appearance the most encompassing and self-sufficient of forms, is uniquely dependent on the texts that precede it—that is, can speak only as the end and consummation of some much longer discourse over the centuries. A second paradox now emerges about epic as a uniquely contingent form: apart from the *Iliad*, epics have credibility only as they come at the end of certain kinds of careers. Even the *Odyssey* was explained by Pseudo-Longinus as the product of Homer's old age. In prose, apprenticeships that advance from short to long, *humilis* to *gravis*, are regular: from short story to novel in Tolstoy's case

and from Joyce's *Dubliners* to *A Portrait of the Artist* to *Ulysses*.
We shall argue much the same for the progression from Gogol's
short stories to "Taras Bulba" to *Dead Souls*. The larger form
can be seen to incorporate and comment on the shorter forms.[60]
With autobiographical or semiautobiographical narratives, the
career then becomes the pilgrimage (Dante's *Commedia*). Far
from becoming juvenilia, these shorter early texts have continuing use in any oeuvre because they explain things about the
culminating masterpiece—the *Aeneid* or *Paradise Lost*—that
the text cannot explain about itself. For these minor forms, like
the pastoral and the georgic, do not so much memorialize some
closed heroic age as mediate between past and present, the
grand and the everyday, the heroic and the political. Hence it
is that readers can find the "true" Virgil in the less encumbered
voice of the *Georgics* or the *Eclogues*, and more Milton in
"Lycidas" than in *Paradise Lost*. The great epics thus do not
speak to their age in isolation but in fact rely on these "satellite"
forms as a kind of buffer, a mode of translating heroic values
to ordinary use in ways that go beyond what the epics themselves
can provide. Gogol's placement of "Taras Bulba" within the
Mirgorod cycle will provide a concrete example of this need to
cushion and insulate the boldest heroic statements.

As with the created memory of "heroic ages," the simplicities imposed on epics—noble to Lukács, dull to Bakhtin—are
themselves an important element in the tradition, for they suggest the field of reader expectations in which writers of epic
operate or which they share. Bakhtin's brief analysis of *Dead
Souls* reflects precisely the misapprehensions of epic that may
have led Gogol himself astray: "The form of his epic Gogol
modeled on the *Divine Comedy*; it was in this form that he
imagined the greatness of his work lay. But what in fact emerged
was Menippean satire. Once having entered the zone of familiar
contact he was unable to leave it, and he was unable to transfer
into this sphere distanced and positive images" ("Epic and
Novel," p. 28). Bakhtin sees in Menippean satire, mixing as it

does prose and poetry, high style and low subjects, an ancient
precursor of the novel, a form that stands in familiar, disre-
spectful proximity to its subjects. What he excludes is that "the
zone of familiar contact," the satirist's underworld, could be the
traditional starting place of cosmic journeys. Yet may it not be
the attempt to leave this fallen world that distinguishes the bard
from the satirist, regardless of whether or not that attempt is
successful? Dante's escape is acknowledged; Milton's remains
controversial (did Satan win?); Gogol burned his sequel and
turned to epistles. Bakhtin continues: "Gogol could not manage
the move from Hell to Purgatory and then to Paradise with the
same people and in the same work; no continuous transition
was possible" (p. 28). Yet what Bakhtin expects of Purgatory,
as of the whole epic landscape, is the stuff not of epic but of
scripture (and of theology more than of scripture). His confusion
is interesting, for it may replicate the literalism that left Gogol
himself forever waiting at the gate: "It [the epic world of the
absolute past] is given solely as tradition, sacred and sacrosanct,
evaluated in the same way by all and demanding a pious attitude
toward itself" (p. 16). But, of course, Dante's mundanely angelic
Purgatory proves accessible precisely because it is such an ambiguous realm, so complexly human. It is not the world of the
absolute past or the coming eternity, but proceeds, as do we,
under the cycles of the sun. There is no angel at the gate, but
Roman Cato; pagan history, myths, and art are not left behind
but continue on, tellingly juxtaposed with biblical. Pagan Virgil
is finally abandoned, but not before Roman Statius has joined
up. The transitional nature of this realm is emphasized stylis-
tically by the degree to which the style is scriptural and non-
scriptural, or rather half-scriptural and entirely epic. To the
large degree that Purgatory is the invention of Dante's own
imagination rather than of Christian theology, it bears its own
self-qualifications as metaphor and is not "given solely as tradition." Indeed, the farther Dante gets from Hell, the less
tradition he has to go on. Purgatory is a poetic realm charac-

terized by all the complicated give-and-take with contemporary reality—of spirit into flesh—that Bakhtin excludes for the epic and that Gogol himself may never have grasped as appropriate for the redemptive mode of his *commedia*. Hardest of all to portray is a second birth that is a rebirth into flesh, a promotion to humility: "Gogol lost Russia, that is, he lost his blueprint for perceiving and representing her; he got muddled somewhere between memory and familiar contact—to put it bluntly, he could not find the proper focus on his binoculars" (p. 28). To be sure, there is a muddle between the grubby particulars of Gogol's provincial N—— and the vast shadow cast by a once and future Rus', but can we be sure that it is not a designed muddle?—that the blurring shift of focus, the near suddenly seen from afar, is not one of the characteristic effects of epic?

In *Selected Passages* Gogol, like Bakhtin, is a theorist trying to explain why the narrative of *Dead Souls* stalled after the first installment. As noted above, his history of Russian poetry centers on a notion of heteroglossia very like Bakhtin's, and equally teleological. The penultimate chapter of *Selected Passages*, on the originality of Russian verse, is Gogol's literary posing of the question Whither Rus'? Yet Gogol reverses Bakhtin's direction almost exactly. The lack of a monumental center is not a liberation but a captivity. Having surrendered to the French language and European writers, the Russians do not yet know their own language. It remains hidden, fractured, unresolved:

> Our poets have perceived that the time has not yet come
> to paint us as a whole and brag about us, that we must
> still be organized, become ourselves and make ourselves
> Russians. Our nature is still too soft, still too unpre-
> pared to take the form fitting to it; we have still not had
> time to take in the total of that multitude of elements of
> all kinds and all origins brought into our land from
> every place, an incoherent concurrence of alien forces

within us, an unwise result of a concatenation com-
manded by God. (*Selected Passages*, p. 243)

The inchoate diffuseness of Russian culture is a form of Babel,
and Gogol moves to the final chapter, "Easter Sunday," with a
vision of the descent of the Holy Spirit that recalls the reversing
of Babel at Pentecost:

This [true Russian] speech will pass into every soul, it
will not fall on sterile soil. Our poetry will be imbued
with an angelic passion and, having struck every string
there is in the Russian, it will move the most hardened
soul with a holiness with which no power and no
instrument in man can contend: it will evoke our Russia
for us—our Russian Russia. (p. 248)

Gogol's vision is radically centripetal. It looks, like Pentecost,
to the rescinding of difference, to unification. Here we see clearly
the Gogol who had left himself no human language with which
to work. He was possessed of a theory whose absolute terms
prevented him from speaking at the cultural center—that is,
from giving Russia the monument she wanted—by the assumption that such a center must be unitary, fixed, not just
stable but eternal, not entirely of this earth. His radical insis-
tence on throwing off foreign masters leaves him with no access
to the international tradition that established Greek epic at the
Virgilian center of Roman letters, pagan Virgil as Dante's guide
to the Christian afterlife, and Catholic, Italian Dante himself
as guide to Chichikov's pilgrimage through the dead as it gave
birth to the Russian novel.

Temporal Closure

If the epic tradition cannot be firmly fixed within an "epic
age," it may still confine itself to describing some such thing.
The handling of time has been invoked since Goethe[61] to differentiate epic from other forms—tragedy for Goethe, the novel

for Bakhtin.[62] Epic is said to assume a fully distanced, completed, irrefutably glorious age that is "vollkommen vergangen," an "absolute past." The values of this age are fixed and normative and are not subject to reinterpretation by the anonymous bards who celebrate them. There are, indeed, ancient epics (the *Iliad*) and modern imitations (Gogol's "Taras Bulba") that maintain this distance; but apart from Homer they are rare even in antiquity. The interweaving of the ages of Aeneas and Augustus in the *Aeneid* typifies the etiological mode of epos that may have been dominant even before the *Iliad*.[63] As on other counts, then, the simplicities of the "epic" pole may be delusory.

The forms that replace the epic—tragedy, the novel, and arguably film—deal with the indeterminacy of the present, the "vollkommen gegenwärtig," and the ineluctable subjectivity of perceiving that present as well as of generating values for an everyday world that has not, as in epic, been fossilized into *gloire*. In Bakhtin's formulation, the open-endedness of the novel as a form responds to the open-endedness of history as we experience it. Now, the drift from the one mode to the other does encapsulate much of literary history in the period when the novel has been attaining predominance. Modern literature manifestly concerns itself with contemporary and ordinary things, "low" subjects, to a degree that ancient did not. Yet within both the epic tradition and the novelistic mode we find works that mix these two temporal perspectives and distinguish themselves in important ways along this same axis. Therein lies much of how the *Odyssey* as a sequel sets itself apart from the *Iliad*, for it shifts the focus from battle to marriage and housekeeping, slaves and peasants, the foolishness of taking risks and the glories of one's own backyard. To be sure, the events recounted officially belong to an age as distant and closed as that of the *Iliad*, yet nothing delineates Ithaca as lost or unattainable in quite the way that Troy is. Conversely, some historical novels, like those of Sir Walter Scott, present a kind of temporal closure, an "absolute past," in contrast to the contemporaneity and subjectivity of *Ulysses*, where the pervasive evocation of Homer serves not to distance and separate past and present but to entangle them in poignant confusion. Certain subjects too lowly for the bourgeois sensibilities of the novel can be accommodated precisely to the extent that the novelist aspires to the "high" form of the epic, with its greater interest in myth and fantasy. For it is as part of an enchanted landscape, an escape from urban, middle-class conventionality, that Tolstoy's wise peasants, Platon (Plato) Karataev in *War and Peace* and Platon Fokanich in *Anna Karenina*, emerge to prophesy and redeem, as descendents commonly of Christ as shepherd and the wise Odyssean herdsman, Eumaeus.

In their fullest forms, epics and novels combine both senses of time, and it may not be the proportions that qualify any given work as epic or novelistic, but rather the direction charted between past and present. That is, it is not the lack of connection with the current time that characterizes the epic so much as the appropriation of contemporary realities to create an importance like that of the past, a raid conducted on the present by a grander past. Writers may permit themselves surprising turns on this issue or, to use Bakhtin's image, refocus their binoculars. Dante's first audience might well have been surprised to find something as immemorial as Hades filled with Florentines whom they may have known personally. His larger intention was not to bring great traditional ideas like Heaven and Hell down to the level of daily reality but, on the contrary, ultimately to claim that near and credible reality for the larger eschatological perspective. We must be alert to the possibility that Gogol did not just betray epic in order to look satirically at contemporary Russia but ended up by claiming the satirized countryside for the eternal notion of Rus'.

In respect to the sense of time, one can find this doubleness in all epics after Homer as a result of the double plot discussed above. Even when the action transpires in some decisively closed

age, the allusiveness of the language, the degree to which it
renews rather than remembers what has been said before (or
rather how it has been said), contradicts the whole notion of
closure. Writing as he does, Virgil is a more material reincar-
nation of Homer than Augustus is of Aeneas, for words can be
preserved and reused in a way that power cannot. In all Christian epic, even when the argument declares pagan antiquity to
be a closed chapter, that past culture lives on as a generative
principle in the style. The notion of the Epic Muse baffles the
modern imagination in instructive ways. Does she symbolize
the weighty authority of received tradition, the certification of
accurate memory, or, on the contrary, some liberating access of
inspiration? Does she serve *ars* or *ingenium*? Are her gifts
agelessly fresh or long fossilized? Faced with these contradictions
the epic poet addresses the fixity of the past in a constantly
transmuting poetic medium that itself eludes fixity and even (in
the Grecizing Latin of Roman epic, the Latinate Italian of
Dante, and un-Englished English of Milton) the separate identity of particular languages. Though the novel may be the fruit
of a polyglot era, as Bakhtin observes, it can and usually does
speak in a single language in a way that fully realized epic
cannot. Quite unlike its plot *in illo tempore* (when such it is),
the language of epic is all history and no past—or rather, a
past not remembered but spoken. As is the nature of prose, the
language of the novel ages far more quickly and conspicuously
than the atemporal artificialities of epic discourse. In incorporating epic tones, obsolete as the theorist may find them, the
novel does not become instantly antiquated in its discourse so
much as it strives to agelessness and insulation from its own
passing moment. In other words, anachronism may be an active
defense against obsolescence.

   Novels, like all modern literature, explore subjectivity more
intensively than does ancient poetry. Yet one cannot therefore
claim that the *movement* toward subjectivity is necessarily a
movement away from epic, for in the Christian system the mind

as a place unto itself becomes the true and only site of heroic endeavor, and therefore a fit ground for epic struggles. Confessional literature, starting with Augustine, provides one of the purest embodiments of novelistic tendency. Dante turned it into epic; and no one will claim that he is deficiently confessional or, in Christian terms, deficiently heroic. To deal with this problem, Lukács sees Dante as moving backward and forward simultaneously, for in him "principles of structuration which tend toward the novel are re-transformed back into the epic."[64] As noted above, epic may identify itself in contradistinction to the novel not by the proportions of its temporal and evaluative perspectives, but by the movement among them; not, that is, the net amounts of "high" and "low," "far" and "near," "then" and "now," but by a final redemptive drift (even if it seems only a blurring of focus) that snatches up humbler things to serve higher perspectives, even if those higher views are just questions and muddled hopes.

In adopting this perspective, we shall perhaps be less baffled that the most monumental of novelistic traditions—and by including works like *War and Peace*, *The Brothers Karamazov*, *And Quiet Flows the Don*, and *The First Circle* we can reasonably call it the most epic—should take its beginning from Chichikov's visit to a village of living dead and immense pygmies. For, as we have noted, it is not unprecedented in the epic tradition, or at least around it, for smaller to give birth to larger and mockery to spawn high seriousness, that is, for heterogeneous and "low" materials to coalesce into a larger hope. As we shall see, in some ways this is the argument of *Dead Souls* itself. In presenting epic more as cycle than as genre, as a mode of other genres rather than a form unto itself, we propose a new meaning to the familiar designation of an "epic tradition" in the Russian novel. For it is not just scale and calling that define the category but the quality of memory that attaches the novels to the prophets of other nations—Homer, Virgil, Dante—

and novelist to novelist, as in Dostoevsky's implicit sense that he is not just replicating or rivaling Gogol's vision but materially continuing his project, as we shall see. This is a quality of memory potent enough to transform the view even of proximate, ignoble reality.

As we noted at the outset, using the great bards entails some hidden costs. Once one has invoked Greeks, Romans, and Florentines to drive French books from Russian soil, one may find oneself still culturally enslaved to equally foreign and merely older masters. They may allow the writer to speak for the very origins of civilization, now pristinely recreating themselves on Russian soil, and may validate his prophetic tone. Yet such necromancy is easier to start than to stop, and what may be reexperienced are not just the primal virtues and vigors of Western culture but its first schisms—schisms that call into question the very act of making fictions and other false idols. The conqueror of Parnassus may regret that it was not Zion. Beyond the bards one finds the prophets; behind epic, scripture; behind heroes, patriarchs. The antique perspectives that adroitly celebrate Russian spirituality in contrast to European materialism also evoke the secular, pagan origins of epic. Though more uncontaminated than the current moment, antiquity itself proves to have its better and worse parts.

The journey beyond novelistic fiction may then continue on beyond any fiction whatsoever, as we see in the careers of Tolstoy and Solzhenitsyn in the wake of Gogol, to whom we now turn. Viewed over the shoulder, epic becomes scripture, and this, with surprising frequency, turns out to be what the epic novelists of Russia finally decide that they want to write or to have written. Yet the force and richness of the tradition is also such that the same men as theorists, Russians, or Christians may discuss epic as one thing but write it as quite another, aspire to it as monolith but execute it, necessarily, as mosaic.

GOGOL IN ROME 2

Of Russia I can write only in Rome, only there it stands before me in all its immensity.

> ——N. V. Gogol to P. A. Pletnev,
> March 17, 1842

In July of 1836, amid the stormy reception of *The Government Inspector*, Gogol set off on his first trip to Rome, where he was to spend the better part of the next six years and reach the pinnacle of his career.[1] In time he called the city his spiritual home and Italian his second language. Rome proved to be the site of his greatest productivity, which climaxed in 1842 with the publication of the first part of *Dead Souls*, the premiere of *Marriage*, and a new edition of the Collected Works incorporating "The Overcoat," as well as extensive revisions of "Taras Bulba" and "The Portrait." For a writer finishing a magnum opus intended to put Russia on the literary map (as *Dead Souls* did), Rome was an obvious choice. Winckelmann and Goethe had established an Italian pilgrimage as de rigueur for Romantics.[2] For Russians, the city of Augustus and Saint Peter had long symbolized the national sense both of exclusion and of election—the heart of a Europe toward which they felt both peripheral and, in the vision of Moscow as the third Rome, proprietary. What more appropriate site than the Eternal City for inscribing Russia's great book?[3] Both writer and book (on which he had been working for two years) were to be reborn in this city that, along with the entire country, Gogol anthropomorphized in one of his letters as "a beloved one" and "a beautiful woman." In the same letter he wrote: "[Italy] is mine. No one in the world can take her away from me. I was born here. Russia, Petersburg...were but a dream. I have reawakened and am again in my homeland."[4] Like the real inspector general, who arrives only when the false one has come and gone, the resurrected author and his great salvational novel were to appear directly after the nightmare of Russia had terminated in the spiritually renewing setting of Rome.

Gogol himself compared living in Rome to reading an epic and savored the palimpsestic quality of the city:[5] "One half of it gives off the aroma of the life of paganism, the other half the age of Christianity, and both are the two greatest ideas in the world."[6] His close companion P. V. Annenkov tells us that "he was rereading his favorite passages from Dante, Gnedich's *Iliad*, and Pushkin's poetry"[7]—that is, the wellsprings of monumental literature, respectively, for Christendom, for Europe, and for Russia. In "The Portrait," the Russian monk-painter, whose noble example haunts and finally destroys the corrupt society portraitist Chertkov, made this double pilgrimage to Italy (while Chertkov indulges himself in Petersburg) and to the classics (while Chertkov can affirm only the modern, and finally himself):

> He [the ideal painter] ended up taking for his teacher
> only the divine Raphael, like a great poet who, after
> reading many works of every kind, full of many
> wonderful and sublime passages, leaves Homer's *Iliad* on
> his table as his constant book of reference, having
> discovered that it contains everything one can wish, and
> that there is nothing in the whole world that cannot be
> found in it expressed to perfection. And so he had
> gained from the study of his great master's works a

sublime conception of creative art, an intense beauty of
thought, and the superb loveliness of a divinely inspired
brush.[8]

The classic masters, like the Holy City, bear witness to the
divine even beyond what they as pagans or humanists might
have quite realized. The happy coexistence of Christianity and
paganism in Rome symbolized for Gogol the compatibility,
perhaps the identity, of the classic with the holy.

The result of Gogol's Roman pilgrimage, the first part of
Dead Souls, did succeed in launching a monumental tradition
in Russian prose, as even the French acknowledged, starting
with the Vicomte E.-M. de Vogüé.[9] *Dead Souls*, however, may
be the most problematic text in monumental literature, Russian
or other.[10] Labeling itself a "poèma" (monumental narrative) it
proceeds to be anything but that, until it ends by prophesying
national destiny as if it had been an epic all along. Mangled
traces of Homer, Virgil, Ovid, and Dante are recoverable from
the text and sometimes flaunted by it, but the reader seeking
a national bard senses from the outset that he is being led on
a wild-goose chase. But then, how is Gogol, of all writers, to
affect the massive, dusty solemnities on which such national
monuments repose? His contradictoriness does not stop here,
for even while finishing *Dead Souls* he played the bard quite
differently in other texts: the revision of the 1835 "Taras Bulba"
and the preliminary sketches for a novel, *Annunziata*, published
as "A Fragment" in 1841 and later called "Rome." These two
texts, along with *Dead Souls*, show his first direct address to
national destiny and the individual's role in it. All three devolve
to a narrative dead end that a moment of ecstatic vision then
proclaims to be a beginning. In each case that vision looks out
over an expansive landscape inscribed with Destiny; in each
case the narrator sees more than his fleeing, dying, or swooning
hero. Prophecy thrice gets born from the collapse of plot, and
a heroic narrator springs full-blown from the head of a depleted

protagonist. It is this heroic narrator, a prophet beyond fiction, who, failing to sustain the sequel of *Dead Souls*, resorts to the oracular hysteria of *Selected Passages from Correspondence with Friends* (1847).

What Part One of *Dead Souls*, the 1842 "Taras Bulba," and "Rome" commonly reveal, then, is Gogol at the end of his own fictive capacities even as he is giving the Russian novel its monumental beginning. His career, like *Dead Souls*, sets the pattern for what is to come, for the epic mode of the Russian novel regularly exacts some such price from its masters. Pursued with utmost seriousness, the form leads beyond storytelling to preaching, as with Tolstoy and Solzhenitsyn, or at the least to prophetic vision (Dostoevsky and Pasternak).

"Taras Bulba" and "Rome" interest us here chiefly as they demonstrate Gogol's ambivalences in writing *Dead Souls*, for things dizzyingly mixed in the novel sort themselves out in these two texts, the buoys, as it were, between which Gogol tacks his course in *Dead Souls*. Both "Taras Bulba" and "Rome" derive from the epic tradition, but from opposite parts of it: the one from the epic as a close approach to folk poetry; the other, from the Dantesque elaboration of the form as the ultimate expression of self-consciousness. "Taras Bulba" revives heroic literature in its most severe form—out-Homers Homer—and insists on both historical and narrative closure. The dying Cossack ends an era along with the tale. By contrast, as veiled spiritual autobiography "Rome" continues the tradition of Christian monumental literature established by Saint Augustine and brought to its culmination by Dante, a tradition that pointedly erodes such boundaries by revivifying the past so that it may draw the present backward and upward to itself. The fragment's gestures toward plot get lost in the ecstasy of perceiving: the prince's life matters only as it informs his perceptions, while the Roman past remains immanent in what is seen. The "then" constantly shapes and is shaped by the beholding eye in an inchoate narrative that evolves from romance to bildungsroman to painterly meditation. As we shall see, the structural peculiarity of *Dead Souls* partly explains itself in the shift from one narrative mode to the other—that is, from saga to confession—as closure opens out to immanence and the protagonist gives way to the narrator. Gogol's satire of provincial life by the end turns in on itself to become increasingly an account of consciousness. Though Chichikov is known to us through much of the text only as others perceive him, by the end his consciousness (or something like it) emerges to direct the action and, it almost seems, to tell the tale; he comes very close to becoming the narrator. What starts out as tourism, a veristic account of the provincial countryside, by the end penetrates the national ethos and brings us finally to the central question of national destiny. What sends the troika racing forward at the end is the force of spiritual implosion, as the powerful negativities of the Russian identity finally assert and define themselves.

"Taras Bulba"

Responding to the calls of monumentality and nationality, Gogol, in his 1842 version of "Taras Bulba," lengthened the 1835 tale by a third and supplemented his earlier Ukrainian chauvinism by celebrating the Russian struggle against the barbaric, Europeanizing, and Roman Catholic Poles. He added thirteen Homeric similes and let the dying hero proclaim the Russian destiny.[11] Along with similes, catalogues, epic scene types (warrior assemblies, the view from the wall), and surgically precise gore, Gogol imported the Homeric vision of *kleos*, the warrior immortality that exists only in the lays of bards—here bandura players. The singer's duty is to celebrate and immortalize as simply as the Cossack's is to fight; both groups must commonly denounce and oppose the demonic forces (Poles, Jews, women) in this black-and-white universe. Though the narrative voice does periodically explain the "then" in terms of the "now," until the very end it calls no attention to its· own values or

perceptions and affects a bardic anonymity that allows the tale
to roll relentlessly onward unencumbered by psychology, by
irony, or even by any attempt to recommend the Cossacks'
brutality to the readers' sympathy. Just as the iron-willed Cossacks live and die in a world of fixed values, so the narrative
harbors no question about the use or value of memory.

Yet it is the Homer of bored schoolboys, father of clichés,
who limps across these pages, as if Gogol were imitating his
own demonic painter, Chertkov, who immortalizes his tasteless
clients as Psyche, Mars, or Aphrodite. Cossacks dressed up in
epithets are supposed to become statuesque and classical. The
added similes of "Taras Bulba" distinguish themselves within
the epic tradition only by their utter predictability, one thing
that better bards and worse have managed to avoid. In the
Iliad, of course, the vehicle often has a life of its own and goes
off from the tenor in intriguing ways that lighten the mounting
carnage and freshen a familiar tale. The Virgilian simile, though
not digressive, does, by multiple and exact parallels, compel a
sorting out of the correspondences, some of them subversive of
the text's larger pieties, while the wondrous puzzles of Dante's
comparisons squarely disconcert the single-minded reader.[12] The
similes of "Taras Bulba," however, serve only to aggrandize the
unremarkable into the obvious:

> he quietly planned to rouse them all suddenly with a
> great Cossack cry to chase even better cheer than ever
> back into their hearts—something of which only the
> broad, mighty Slavonic soul is capable, a soul that is to
> others what the sea is to shallow rivers. If the tempest
> blows, it howls and thunders and surges and throws up
> colossal waves such as powerless streams can never raise;
> but when it is calm, it is clearer than any river and
> spreads its glassy surface to the horizon, soothing the
> eyes that gaze upon it. (p. 316)[13]

This analogy simply amplifies, concretizes, and implies as natural some threadbare chauvinism. Without individuating detail

(what river? what sea? whose eyes?) the image elicits no precise and pleasurable visualization. It does not jog the mind but lulls it. Yet a look at Gogol's earlier and quirkily brilliant remakings of Homeric similes suggests how well he could rival the vigor and raw unpredictability of epic comparisons when he was not, as in "Taras Bulba," attempting a textbook imitation of them. Compare this simile from "A Terrible Vengeance":

> then the Dnieper is terrible to behold! Its surging waves
> roar as they pound against the hills, then retreat
> glistening and sighing, and weep and lament in the
> distance. Thus does the old Cossack mother weep and
> wail as she bids farewell to her soldier son. Full of high
> spirits he spurs on his sable steed, rakishly leaning to
> one side and wearing his cap dashingly aslant; she runs
> after him, sobbing, holding him by the stirrup, catching
> the bridle, and wrings her hands as she sheds torrents of
> bitter tears. (p. 193)

Since Homer's Hecuba and Hector, mothers weeping over departing sons have been inevitable fixtures of epic, and Gogol was to write that cliché into the plot of "Taras Bulba." This river simile, however, turns convention upside down. Where classical similes typically figure human reactions in terms of nature (for example, eyes like blazing fire), Gogol reverses the process by comparing the river to human behavior, indeed, a highly particular example thereof. The pathetic fallacy thus acquires, as it rarely does, dramatic specificity. As often in Homer, the parallels remain problematical: "A Terrible Vengeance" in fact has no Cossack mother dispatching her son. The simile adds to the perplexing nexus of family relationships in the tale and, in further personifying the Dnieper, elaborates the projection into that river of human personality, demonic will, or perhaps both. The Dnieper in this story is only the most complex working out of a motif developed throughout *Evenings on a Farm near Dikanka*, the river as a mirror concealing the inner, hidden, perhaps satanic realities of the soul, the very symbol of the unseen. But when the Dniester provides the culminating image of the 1842 "Taras Bulba," Gogol excludes everything below that glassy surface and makes the river a monolithic symbol of Russian character:

> The Dniester is a fair-sized river, with many inlets, rushy patches, sandbanks and deep pools; its mirroring surface shines and echoes the call of the swans, the proud golden-eye duck glides across it, and a host of snipes, red-cropped ruffs and all kinds of other birds hide in its reeds and on its banks. The Cossacks sailed swiftly in the narrow boats, plying the oars together, steering clear of the sandbanks, startling the birds, and speaking of their ataman. (p. 353)

The familiar pun on Gogol's own name in "golden-eye duck"[14] invites many interpretations, but one of the most attractive, given the obviousness and simplicity of the heroic scene, is to see the author himself for once simply gliding over the glassy surface of things (though, as we shall see, this self-consciousness itself does ruffle the surface). In the technique, then, as in the substance of "Taras Bulba," Gogol has for once resisted his penchant for stepping through the looking glass and, taking epic directness as an excuse for viewing the world as pure surface, has subjugated Cossacks, similes, and his own persona to the overriding imperatives of Russia and Orthodoxy.

Epic thus distilled ceases to be epic, and in both versions "Taras Bulba" conspicuously lacks the ability to stand on its own.[15] Epic, for all of the gods and national destinies that it has served, may be the least monolithic of forms. Its great scope can accommodate something like a fair fight among the various principles at play, as no text demonstrates better than *Dead Souls* itself. The *Iliad*, amid all its glory-mongering, also and oppositely denounces war as has never been done since; Homer blames no one for being Trojan, and his cruel, randomizing

Olympians unwittingly shepherd all afflicted mortals toward a common sympathy. Unlike tragedy, for example, it creates space within a single text for the Achilles that kills Hector and the Achilles that welcomes Priam. Virgil's Rome comes triumphantly to birth amid a primeval landscape that might have thrived better without her, and in the invasion of Italy, as at Homer's Troy, we can feel on both sides of the battle. Milton, as Blake speculated, may have been of the Devil's party without knowing it. And though Dante distilled the essence of Christendom, he did so as an exile, and at moments as a heretic.

Whatever epic affirms, then, it affirms only on balance and with gallant regard for the losing side. "Taras Bulba," admitting no ambiguities, deflates such nobility by mean-spirited abuse of the enemy. The seduction of the younger son by a Polish beauty and his betrayal of his father constitute a tragic plot only in the most superficial sense. The inner conflicts of the participants, even those of Taras in executing his son, scarcely figure. That the younger and more aesthetic of the sons should be the weak link in the chain seems entirely inevitable and devoid of irony. In denying any currents under the mirrored surface, Gogol excludes both tragedy and the latent restorative powers of comedy. The primitivism of "Taras Bulba" seeks to revive the folklore prior to either mode. Yet the strong, simple, manly truths here uttered sound more like those of boys deploying tin soldiers about a cardboard field.

Already the 1835 story, however, is a simple text in a complex position. "Taras Bulba" stands as the second tale in the *Mirgorod* cycle, four contrasted views of the Russian past that variously explore what we may call the satellite forms of epic. These forms include the pastoral, the georgic, and the mock epic, all of which treat the heroic world, but without the closure toward which epic finally tends; that is, they constantly mediate between the "then" and the "now," the large and small, the heroic and the everyday, by locating themselves in some fantastic middle distance.

Poggioli has discussed the first story in the cycle, "Old World Landowners" as a pastoral, or rather as a deformation of pastoral.[16] The narrator's most extensive philosophical intrusion into the text, before the black cat somehow dooms Pulkheria, seems programmatic both for the tale and the cycle:

> Some conqueror rallies all his country's forces, wages war for several years, his generals cover themselves with glory, and it all ends with the acquisition of a patch of land on which there is barely room to plant potatoes; while sometimes two sausage-makers have a fight over some trifle and in the end their quarrel spreads over cities, big and small villages and finally, the whole kingdom.[17]

Remembering this digression, the reader will at the very least see the heroic simplifications of "Taras Bulba" in more complex terms. This observation, which of course will find a large working out in the historical philosophy of *War and Peace*, descends from Virgil's scheme for the *Eclogues*, "to compare large things with small" (1.23), by way of the mock-heroic assumption that proportions in the world are hopelessly confused. It does much to explain Gogol's puzzling comparison of Afanasii and Pulkheria, human vegetables, to the rustic nobility of Ovid's Philemon and Baucis.[18] The point is that in this topsy-turvy world, the large has been trivialized—man becomes merely a mouth— and the trivial, the mere act of eating, takes on the appearance of a consuming, world-controlling passion. The traditional catalogue of heroes has become a monumental menu, as in *Dead Souls* it will become a listing of the contents of Chichikov's trunk. This passage captures the once and future Gogol in a moment of transition. The fatal cat typifies the peripeties of his earlier short stories, where the demonic suddenly irrupts into a world of dull routine, a plot that Gogol is abandoning. The orderly epic universe toward which he now moves suffers disruption only from the tamperings of Olympians or the invisible hand of national destiny. Invoking the strong sense of scale and proportion of that epic view, Gogol here manages to see the sinister cat as a form of mock-heroic overthrow. As we shall see, the resulting tone, at once demonic and deflating, in fact will play a large role in *Dead Souls*.

Later, in *Mirgorod*, the agon of the two Ivans, faded epigones of Cossackdom, similarly epitomizes triviality, a mock-heroic battle of legal memos. Here the dominant concerns of "Taras Bulba"—militarism, comradeship, orthodoxy—show up as sordid miniatures,[19] yet in a way that somehow generates a genuine sense of tragedy at the end. Similarly, "Viy" begins with an overtly mock-heroic battle of the various orders (that is, classes) of seminarians with their pompous titles: "Then Philosophy would go to war, with their long black moustaches, and last of all Theology, in their baggy trousers and with their beefy necks" (p. 356). In calling his protagonist, Khoma Brut, "the philosopher," the narrator provides the seminarian with a comically oversized title that nonetheless deepens the allegory of a tale seriously involved with the nature of evil. Like the pastoral pleasance and the mock-heroic barnyard, Gogol's Ukraine exists in the middle distance, described to an urbane audience by a self-conscious narrator yet overshadowed in the background by an earlier and lost heroic age, Cossackdom. Virgil's poetic herdsmen similarly find themselves somewhere between Troy and Augustan Rome, Achilles and the divine Caesar. Both the lost heroic grandeur and the author's urbanity are necessary for providing scale to the descriptions.

"Taras Bulba," then, provides the cycle with the heroic standard against which the forces of burgeoning decline can be judged in the other tales. By holding simplistically to the most conventional sense of heroic grandeur, the tale provides a foil for the tricks of proportion in the other tales. Similarly, Virgil set off his bucolics by including toward the middle of the collection the "Messianic" Fourth Eclogue, a fully prophetic and patriotic piece against which the much more ambiguous

surrounding pieces can be judged. In much the same way, the
great epics after Homer regularly include condensed reminders
of traditional militarism to provide scale for their real subject,
some new and more complex form of heroism. In making this
comparison, flashing armor becomes a shorthand for a simpler
past. Apollonius gives his Argonauts a battle or two at the start
of their voyage as a foil for his innovative depiction of the
warfare of love between Jason and Medea. Virgil includes some
bloodthirsty Greeks (Pyrrhus, Diomedes) to clarify what is noble
and onerous in the new Trojan-Roman heroism. The firebrand
Ulysses in *Inferno* 26 sets off the vast wickedness of Satan, and
Milton's War in Heaven prepares us for the subtler battle waged
in Eden. Although Dante's Ulysses and Milton's Satan capture
and hold some readers' imaginations, these epics mean to keep
us marching past the old glories to a more complex set of values.
Collections like the *Eclogues* and *Mirgorod*, with the contrast-
ings of old and new, high and low, present similar dangers to
the reader who stops short or excerpts. It is no fairer to judge
Virgil's radically ambivalent view of Augustus's Rome and of
heroic literature from his Fourth Eclogue than it is to judge
Gogol's view of Russia from "Taras Bulba," though audiences
have misread and cherished both pieces in isolation from the
surrounding cycles.

   Mirgorod as a cycle suggests that already in 1835 Gogol
was aware that the deformations of the heroic (sentimentally as
something like the pastoral, comically as mock-heroic), for which
he had particular talent, were hindered by the lack of an evolved
heroic tradition in Russia. There being no other monument for
him to chip away at, he provided one himself. If readers otherwise lack an Achilles in Russian garb, let them read "Taras
Bulba." Is it surprising, then, that in 1842 *Dead Souls*, as a
yet larger assault on the heroic vanities of the culture, should
be in need of a yet bigger foil and therefore confront a potentially
hostile audience in tandem with an even more monumental and
strident "Taras Bulba"? If readers do not know what the crazy,

proliferating Homeric similes of *Dead Souls* are parodying, let
them look at the thirteen new ones in "Taras Bulba." Gogol's
heroic text thereby makes possible the ironies of *Dead Souls* by
supplying the normative tradition from which it can then proceed
to make the most inventive deviations.

Gogol may also have aimed to mollify as well as educate
the Russian audience by this text. Proffer has recently argued
that "Taras Bulba," along with other 1842 works, "Departure
from the Theater" and the revision of "The Portrait," serves
to protect the author from the doubts about his patriotism and
artistic seriousness that he knew *Dead Souls* would inevitably
provoke.[20] These works allow him a measure of patriotic and
artistic self-certification to bolster the apologia offered by the
authorial voice in the final chapters of *Dead Souls*.[21] In these
shorter works of 1842, especially in "The Portrait," he articulates a redemptive vision where the artist, through self-purifi-
cation and denial, enables himself to turn even the meanest
subject matter to pedagogical purpose. As we mentioned at the
start, the artist-monk who retreats to Italy to perfect his own
art in contrast to the hapless Chertkov provides a particularly
flattering image of Gogol's own Roman pilgrimage.

If "Taras Bulba" is a gesture to the national audience, it
is a guilty gesture, and one whose exaggerations of epic technique
establish how unnatural they were to the author. It could well
be that, in order to get from the phantasmagoria of the short
stories with their exquisite normlessness to the orderly or at
least potentially organizable cosmos of monumental literature,
Gogol might for once have designed a universe where norms
prevailed to the exclusion of personality. Even this saga does
not end without puncturing those orderly surfaces, however. The
golden-eye duck on the glassy surface of the final river is, after
all, the author's pun on himself, a signature on the canvas such
as bards are strictly not allowed. That Taras himself dies a good
deal more complexly than he has lived compromises the tale's
strong principles of closure. For his final concussion not only

induces second sight, but a notion of Russia and nationhood glimpsed centuries too early.

In any case, true epic heroes are not prophets, even at the stake; that role properly falls to Teiresias and Merlin, along with various ghosts and angels. Heroes regularly grasp only with difficulty the history that they are shaping. The meaning that Gogol imposes here compensates for the plot's failure to show Taras's own action as leading to his demise and thereby to reveal his greatness as it self-destructs. It is no tragic decision that fells him, but age, obsolescence, the movement of history, a lost pipe. That he should fall victim to the standard decaying universe of heroic poetry makes it all the more anachronistic for him to foresee progress, unification, and autonomy. It is not the Poles who do him in, but a narrator who has run out of episodes and wants to derive more meaning from this tale than it has quite supplied.

"Rome"

On first view, "Rome" seems as private and self-indulgent as "Taras Bulba" is stiffly official. Where "Taras Bulba" presents a view of an absolute past that is fixed, complete, and not subject to reinterpretation or diminution of its spiritual authority, "Rome" views the past as entirely immanent in the present moment and contingent on the receptivity of the observer. In short, Gogol's fragment offers a near literary antithesis to the flatness, stolid heroism, and historical closure of "Taras Bulba." Gogol claimed that it appeared in 1841, largely against his wishes, in payment of a debt, though its inclusion in the 1842 Collected Works suggests less abashment about its publication.

Gogol's descriptions of Rome closely parallel the letters he wrote home, as Richter has established,[22] and show the author shunning his monumental vocation for more private and aesthetic fantasies. He transparently veils his spiritual tourism with the fiction of a Roman prince, educated abroad, who returns

to see his city through fresh and historically informed eyes. For
Baroti, who has studied Dantesque motifs in Gogol's tale, the
prince's four-year stay in Paris and his subsequent disillusion-
ment can be compared to the misguided Dante's state of confusion and loss of moral foundation at the beginning of the
Inferno.[23] Not surprisingly, then, a Beatrice-figure, Annunziata
from Albano,[24] waits offstage to consummate his spectatorship;
but the narrative leaves off as the nobleman prepares his approach to her. An actual encounter with this madonna would
obviously unsettle the fantasy of a life purged of other annoy-
ances (authority figures, money problems, friends, and artistic
talent) and compromise the protagonist's rapturous passivity. It
would scarcely do for the redeemer in the piece to intrude more
than does the tyrannical father, who dispatches his timorous
son to Paris at the moment when he would have wished to go
and then obligingly dies to bring him back when the city's
Parisian excitements prove hollow. As nowhere else in Gogol's
fiction, Russia does not figure in this tale, nor do the burdens
of prophecy. The Eternal City has seen too many laureates to
need more at this point; it welcomes artists, but observers will
do. Gogol's Rome, then, is a literary world on holiday from the
issues that otherwise vex him. The faint gestures to plot give
way to his most extensive portrayal of a single (and positive!)
character's psychology, even though the nobleman's inner world
involves little beyond connoisseurship. Whereas the heroic world
is all mythos, an unstoppable chain of events, "Rome" restricts
itself to the novelistic world of observation and self-creation.
The episodes of this fragment hang together no more tightly—
and perhaps less interestingly—than do the short story collections, but their unification around a single personality in a
biography-cum-monologue makes a bridge to the continuities of
Dead Souls.

As the text nowhere admits, however, it is a Russian tourist
who is writing, and one intent on taking this utopia home with
him.[25] Just as the titillations of Paris opened the prince's eyes

to the timeless values of his own city, though now a backwater, so Gogol, anticipating his own homecoming, presents Rome as spiritual preparation, a prototype for the Third Rome.[26] Moscow and Rome are both excluded from the faddish and atheistic Europeanness of which Paris is capital, since the pope has shielded his city from the Enlightenment, which Russia also missed. Emperors and popes have come and gone, but the *popolo romano* endures as a counterpart to Russian collectivism. The vitality and essential orderliness of the state derive from the Romans' creative and stable anarchy, a political form whose essential formlessness precludes the kind of revolution *à la française* that the Russians had reason to fear. Having not only seen but caused so much of European history, the Romans now find themselves beyond the inflammatory issues that ignite wars elsewhere. The rich, jumbled accumulation of pagan and Christian monuments resists sorting out; by analogy, the doctrinal differences of Catholicism and Orthodoxy also lose their urgency, even as Gogol's letters in this period reveal a flirtation with the Roman church quite opposite to the orthodoxy of "Taras Bulba."[27] His prince perceives secular France as the antithesis of his homeland, as did Slavophiles. In this godless, materialistic age, provincialism becomes a sign of spiritual election. By the pastoral logic that links the center and the margins and puts kings in particular sympathy with shepherds and fishermen, the Roman sense of being so central to history as to be beyond it recalls the Russian sense of being outside it. The king is not a citizen, and Rome is no more part of Europe than Russia is. Rather, Rome and Moscow stand as the once and future capitals of a Christendom that lies beyond that secularized Europe. Their strength commonly lies in the people, in the earth, in the respect for tradition, in latent vigors apparent only to the prophetic artist.

"Rome" merges two views of history that figure in *Dead Souls*. The first is history as comedy, a natural outgrowth of the collectivist perspective. The comic sense of the Ukrainian

short stories had found little that was redemptive in the steady
decline they chart. But in Rome, the decline and fall of everything in sight reassures and inspires the observer, leading, as it
does, to a superior grade of ruins. No building is complete until
the perfecting hand of nature has covered it with moss. The
lime burners have turned boring imperial symmetries into in-
vitingly broken facades. Where a romantic might give way to
tragic thoughts on loss and the vanity of human wishes, Gogol
sees ruin as the ideal human setting and the ultimate symbol
of human community. For the principle of decline (which spares
the self-regenerating *popolo*) functions like a millennial humor-
ist, bringing the great ages down to the level of the current
inhabitants. The age-old dialectic of natural force and human
artifice resolves itself as moss and erosion mute the hard edges
of human designs.

What it all adds up to is an Eden after, not before, history,
and a better paradise for lacking the fatal choices of the first
garden. The collapsed facades and slow-grinding mills of history
have united appearance and substance, punctured the vanities
of power, but proved the durability of the race. The realities
lurking in the inner, terrifying under-river world of Gogol's
Ukrainian landscapes have now emerged into the bright light
of day; the demons glimpsed there must now learn to take their
place among the legions of other gods, spirits, ghosts, and saints
who claim space in the city. The aesthetics of rot perfected in
the Ukrainian stories now become a principle of historical continuity, and the faded Cossacks of those tales find much more
positive counterparts in the Roman streets. The factotum Peppe,
for instance, is the degeneration of so many different possibilities
from the republican, imperial, Christian, and medieval periods
that the issue can scarcely be raised. He is simply a Roman, a
type that has been declining for so long and with so little
apparent impairment that the whole notion of decadence is called
into question. Decline itself, that is, may be in the eye of the
beholder. The effect reverses that of mock heroic, for the present

is not a betrayal and cheapening of lost glory but a rich outgrowth of it.

By the logic of that perception, all historiography aspires to autobiography, the second and more influential view of history in the tale. On such a note the fragment ends with Gogol's prince (or is it the narrator? the two have now merged) swept away by a prospect of the city: "Lord, what a vision! Seized by it, the Prince forgot himself and the beauty of Annunziata, the secret destiny of his people, and everything else which existed on earth."[28] What can finally terminate this series of descriptions is the paradisiacal self-actualization of the observer in the completed ecstasy of observing. The nobleman has felt vague stirrings about the Beatrice figure, as well as about his responsibility to the destiny of his people, but these tangible externals would only impede the convergence of observer and observed here achieved. Annunziata, did she but know it, has served her function as spiritual guide by leading to something beyond herself. History has figured in the narrative only as handmaiden to the self-perfecting eye, a means of feeling the Roman landscapes more perfectly. The city becomes utopian as the young man learns to perceive it as such, and its triumphs and defeats become real to him as they inform the disposition of marble and moss. Indeed, his intuitions about its lurking powers of renascence may only express his own gestating powers of perception. What ends the narrative, as in "Taras Bulba" and *Dead Souls*, is an observing consciousness that has perfected its passivity into an omnipotent will to perceive, leading to the capacity to confer absolute value on what it perceives. The final accommodation of history, even the endless eventfulness of the Eternal City, to individual responsibility is in the shattering of boundaries, a mystical absorption of the observer into the observed that issues in prophecy. There is no absolute "then," only a constantly unfolding present.

With all of the open-endedness of a journal, "Rome" eludes closure as deftly as "Taras Bulba" imposes it. The several

narrative false starts, however, lead to the visionary conclusion
far more efficiently than "Taras Bulba" and *Dead Souls* do to
theirs. The visionary voice that intrudes to end and valorize the
other two narratives here has held center stage from the first.
Whereas Chichikov and his narrator, like Bulba and the bard,
end up awkwardly yoked together, here the protagonist and the
narrator have merged. Writer and audience did stand apart
from the prince as he succumbed to Parisian sham, but the
overwhelming spectacle of Rome reduces the several perspectives
to only one. That single view is at once the solipsism of the
travel diary and, thanks largely to Dante, the capping epiphany
of Christian epic. Gogol's fictionalization of himself as the Roman prince, by virtue of its various denials—not a Russian,
not an artist, not crazy, not sexually peculiar, not finally either
rich or needy, not even named—presents an inchoate Everyman
that temporarily invites the rest of humanity into the author's
fantasies. Thereby Gogol may almost inadvertently lapse into
his monumental vocation in the very process of momentarily
escaping it; for, in making the private world of fantasy coextensive with the cosmos of national destiny, "Rome" sets the
pattern for *Dead Souls*. At the midpoint of this world the Roman
prince exemplifies, in briefer and more autobiographical terms,
the kind of featureless catalyst, at once dreaming and dreamt,
that at base Chichikov is.

Between them, "Taras Bulba" and "Rome" suggest the
two paths that Gogol, as he was writing the first part of *Dead
Souls*, saw opening to him as he approached Parnassus. Both
works acknowledge, as did his Roman pilgrimage, the necessity
of responding to the very heart of the European tradition—
Homeric epic and the Eternal City, respectively. Both presume
that human experience can be organized in terms of the identity
of a people—not the family or village nor Christendom or mankind, but Rome and Russia. Both acknowledge that preceding
heroic ages prepare and define national identities, though the
historical record is as much an open book in "Rome" as it is

closed and immutable in "Taras Bulba." Both works presume
a radical simplification of the writer's subject matter and of his
social role.

In "Taras Bulba" the needs of history authorize the writer
to see only the broad outlines, the magnificent surfaces of things.
To the audience he sings as faceless bard in the tradition of
Russian saga; they, in turn, can be expected to honor and enjoy
the tale and, through it, their own Russianness. "Rome" turns
just as steeply to solipsism, as if intended for no audience other
than the author. Exactly unlike "Taras Bulba," "Rome" presents history as such infinite and still-evolving complication that
one can only relax and enjoy the constantly mutating sense of
pattern, a response as purely aesthetic as that of "Taras Bulba"
is fundamentally political. Much of the riddle of *Dead Souls*,
Part One, explains itself in the movement from the one world
to the other, that is, from the fixed values and materialism of
"Taras Bulba" (seen now with the humorous distancing found
in the surrounding tales of *Mirgorod*) to the transformative
vision of "Rome," from a world of inevitable decline to the
gestation of a new, spiritually potent nationhood. Though the
reference points for this axial shift, Homer and Dante, blur and
confuse each other in *Dead Souls*, "Rome" and the revised
"Taras Bulba" demonstrate Gogol's ability to confront each
squarely and separately.

Dead Souls, *Part One*

"Taras Bulba" and "Rome" share another characteristic
that sets them apart from Gogol's other early work, their comparative lack of irony. They lack it for opposite reasons but to
much the same effect: the observer is too far from the Cossacks
and, finally, too identified with the Roman prince to allow
Gogol's usual irony to distance and dismiss the subject matter
even while making it too sticky to put down. In these two cases
the narrator does not conspiratorially take the audience aside

with him to laugh and fear together. The customary dissonances and contradictions of Gogol's perspective—his unnerving feel for grotesqueries in which the audience, like the author, must see both absurdity and themselves—are flattened by the statuesque objectivity of the Cossack saga, then evaporate into the solipsism and self-creating subjectivity of "Rome." That is, anyone who is not a Cossack or an expatriate Russian writer will not feel the familiar seduction and betrayal of Gogolian irony, that process of being drawn into the fiction but also set grandly above it and then left wondering who was the real target.

Both tales suspend Gogol's usual ambivalence: "Taras Bulba," through total submission to patriotism and inherited form; "Rome," by casting off Russian subjects and responsibilities. Both of these texts proclaim visions that they cannot begin to explain, for as essentially static narrative forms they will not bear further extension. What makes the Cossacks staunch is their resistance to change, their superhuman voracity for risk and repetition. If the pieties of "Taras Bulba" were taken further, the whole structure would risk seeming a joke. Similarly, beyond the achieved stasis of the observer observed in the act of observing, "Rome" could not proceed further with any claims to having a plot; the narrative has imploded.

What "Taras Bulba" and "Rome" indelibly illustrate is that Gogol, raising his sights to larger topics—from the village to the nation and to Christendom—had a sure feel for the limits of the available forms. Leaving the inward, autobiographical pressures of "Rome" to seek their natural if quick conclusion, he did not attempt to string out enough narrative to sustain the planned *Annunziata*. He revised "Taras Bulba" to be more intensely and identifiably Homeric but did not inflate it into a full-scale epic. In leaving these simpler visions as fragments, Gogol implicitly acknowledged that neither the Homeric nor the Dantesque poles of epic writing could sustain his ambitions. The way toward his chef d'oeuvre had to lie through some mixture of modes, somewhere in the more complicated middle ground of his usual evasive perspectives, but now applied more extensively and on a larger theme. Conflated, these two monumental modes create, explosively, the irony that each of them lacks in its polarized form. The tone that emerges from the first part of *Dead Souls* is neither the aestheticism of "Rome" nor the dispassionate historicizing of "Taras Bulba" but a perspective that transforms itself through repeated escapes from the reader. In that unfolding game, played with shifting rules, the narrator creates himself as bard, and the eluded audience becomes constituted as Russia, the very thing for which they are imputed to be searching. The final joke on them, as typically in Christian literature when it is ironic, is to deflate their obtuseness in awaiting some target other than themselves, in dumbly expecting to be merely the spectators of this satire rather than its true objects. As noted above, the irony of Gogol's early stories had the tendency to turn on the reader even as *The Inspector General* turns on its audience—that is, to include a mirror in the rogues' gallery so that the reader suddenly glimpses himself in bad company. *Dead Souls* returns to that technique, but now with higher stakes.

From the looming "Poèma" of the title page to the concluding hymn to Rus', the narrating voice of *Dead Souls* recurrently invites the audience to attend to his tale as the "epic" that it seems so obviously not to be. A text scuttering insignificantly through the immense shadow of epic verse automatically qualifies as mock-heroic. The author and his audience, who must know what a "real" epic is and what "real" heroism is, are at first united in looking down on this spectacle from an Olympian height.

This mode of irony in the first chapters of *Dead Souls* is well understood, but before analyzing it further we should anticipate the fact that the book shifts midway to a perspective no less ironic but entirely different. All readers note that after chapter 6 the static catalogue of rogues encountered in the first half, all frozen into their various trivial depravities, awaken and unite to pursue Chichikov or, more importantly, to fantasize about him. Finally, even the bard himself, so aloof in the opening chapters, seems to be having Chichikov's nervous breakdown for him. The unleashing of vast spiritual energy does not figure importantly in classical epic or mockery thereof, but it is the very essence of the ironic counterplot to pagan heroism that is articulated in the Gospels, most clearly in the Fourth. The meek do not inherit the earth without the surprising reversals, the recourse to a higher and less literal perspective, characteristic of ironic plots. Yet now the vantage point is not just the Olympus of sophisticated writer and sophisticated reader looking downward together. In the articulation of Christian heroism, as in mock heroic, the great of this world are not what they seem. However, what exposes and deflates them is no longer just the condescension of author and audience to the subject matter as the *miles gloriosus* trips over his sword or warrior valor adjourns to barnyard or nursery. Rather, proportion derives from the descent into the work of the Creator himself, self-conscious and disguised.

This contrast can be grasped most easily by taking a step back from mock heroic to the *Odyssey* as the masterwork of narrative irony in Greek and comparing it to the Gospels. In both, the true king restores his kingdom by traveling first among beggars and peasants. He is heroized by abuse and veils his messages for those who have ears to hear them, so that, as in any ironic vision, literalists cannot be saved. Penelope's suitors, like the scribes and the Pharisees, doom themselves by taking things at face value and failing to note that their underlings— beggars, youths, slaves, and women—may be more powerful than themselves. In the Gospels, however, the leap of faith, guile, or irony that it takes to get beyond literalism is needed not just to win the Kingdom but (probably) to experience it, for it may well be not an earthly kingdom at all. The *Odyssey*'s restored Ithaca will be as concrete and as free of disguise as it

was in the good old days. Though hopes varied, the New
Jerusalem boded well to be something quite different from the
Old. Therein the Christian and classical ironists part company.
Both climax their stories in a moment of revelation and revolution—apocalypse and *anagnōrisis*, respectively—but Christian
writers work away from locating the new dispensation in the
ordinary reality from which the tale took its beginning. The
distance from the Gospels is yet greater in the case of mock-
heroic irony, which works at the expense of the protagonist and
not (as in the *Odyssey*) just his enemies. The added complexity
and instability of such irony are even less capable of suggesting
a vision of a transformed reality. Indeed, when used most
vigorously (for example, by Aristophanes and Pope), it needs
the anchor of the author's own time and place.

As we shall see, in *Dead Souls* Gogol in some ways recapitulates this progression from pagan to Christian by moving
from one type of descent to another. The mock-heroic condescension to the subject matter up through chapter 6 becomes
the creator's descent into his creation to redeem it by incarnating
himself—taking a voice, becoming a character, and thereby
shouldering the burden of human frailty. The tones of perse-
cution heard from the narrator at the end seem oddly uncalled
for until we ponder the tradition of martyrdom and salvation
from which he himself nervously descends.

To trace this movement, we must revert to the opening
ironies of this self-declared and self-deflated "poèma" and to
that other descent of the ironist, his literary genealogy, about
which Gogol, like any good epic writer, solemn or playful, gives
us abundant indication. Quite early we learn that it is not one
but several forms of epic that *Dead Souls* at various times and
in various ways fails to be. Even between the extremes evoked
in "Taras Bulba" and "Rome," Gogol's posthumous "Textbook
of Literature for Russian Youth" presents another category,
"lesser epic," which accommodates *Dead Souls* next to *Orlando*

furioso and *Don Quixote* at one remove from Homer and heading toward the novel.[29] In this form, an unremarkable and limited protagonist usefully symbolizes his age. This mixed form, narratively fantastic and psychologically acute, goes back at least as far as Ovid, whom Gogol occasionally acknowledges ("such a transformation will overtake our Prometheus as even Ovid himself could never think of," p. 39)[30] and pervasively imitates. Operating in the shadow of the titanic Homer and Virgil, Ovid recast epic as a monumental form constantly mutating into brilliant, teasing particulars. His *Metamorphoses* presents a mythic landscape stripped of proportion, fixity, or stable grandeur, where one can rely only on the propensity of beings to turn into something else. As we discussed in chapter 1, one must not assume that such insouciance about epic *gloire* lacks an argument, for in fact the almost hidden path through Ovid's lush imagistic jungle does, convincingly or not, lead us from creation of the world to the glory of Rome in fifteen books.

Rus' is as much a telos of Gogol's tale as Rome is of Ovid's, and the landscape of the first half of *Dead Souls*, Part One, is itself constantly involved in similar metamorphoses. Chapter 1 begins with a doggedly close veristic description, then jars the sense of scale with an intrusion from a now defunct heroic world, a boot, in fact, "of such gigantic proportions that its equal was hardly to be found anywhere, especially in these times, when heroic bogatyrs are beginning to die out even in Russia" (p. 10). The image descends from the Homeric motif of rocks so heavy that three or four men of the current generation could not lift them (*Iliad* 12.445ff.). Among the playfully heroized ranks of children, animals, and boots, even bureaucrats can figure, as for example when one of them becomes in Chichikov's eyes "like ancient Zeus of Homer, who prolonged the days or sent quick-passing nights whenever the need arose either to bring to a close a martial contest between the heroes he liked or to permit them to fight to a finish" (p. 122).

In the *Metamorphoses*, Ovid, like Ariosto, Cervantes, and
Sterne to follow, shrinks and refracts epic into endless variations,
including the pastoral and mock-heroic forms that engage Gogol
particularly in the *Mirgorod* cycle, sometimes from Ovidian
sources, as we have seen. *Dead Souls* uses these various styles
in its first half, though only long enough to suggest that something else is afoot. Manilov's absorption by the Epicurean virtues
of tranquility, friendship, and pipe dreams recapitulates the
amiable retirement from heroic engagement characteristic of the
pastoral. He and his wife enjoy a less fattening version of the
courtly otherworldliness of Afanasii and Pulkheria in "Old
World Landowners" (and Philemon and Baucis before them).
Within this vegetal existence it is the children (as in "Viy")
who embody the mock-heroic principle of disorder in assaulting
each other and dismembering toy soldiers. Their very names
trivialize heroic myth: "Alcides" is the patronymic of the vo-
racious Hercules, perhaps a telling reflection of Manilov's own
gluttony. Themistoclius bears a bungled Latinization of the
Athenian statesman, hero, and (perhaps) turncoat Themisto-
cles—a bad omen for Manilov's ambition that his son become
a diplomat. Gogol's pervasive joke, as often Ovid's, is to provide
an undignified good time in the guise of an "epic."

The mock-heroic joke starts on the title page. In response
to the censors' relegation of the intended title to a subtitle under
"Chichikov's Journeys" (to avert the oxymoronic blasphemy of
implying that souls can die), Gogol buried both titles under the
monumental label "poèma." As a complement to and reversal
of Pushkin's "novel in verse," *Eugene Onegin*, labeling a prose
narrative "poèma" may well declare indebtedness and inde-
pendence in respect to Gogol's mentor, who had suggested the
anecdotal plot. Above all, "poèma," especially for an audience
gratified by "Taras Bulba," could only excite false expectations
about the work to follow. Marching through the facade, one is
surprised to find what looks at first like a rubbish heap. The
narrator continues to present this bagatelle as something ep-

ochal, until in the second half it actually becomes so, if only by opening up voids into which consciousness can flood.

The Homeric similes that proved oppressively serious in "Taras Bulba" here return with splendid, deflating lunacy. At the outset Chichikov enters town society at the Governor's ball:

> Upon entering the main hall Chichikov was compelled to
> narrow his eye for a minute or so, since the brilliance of
> the candles and lamps and the ladies' gowns was terrific.
> Everything was flooded with light. Everywhere one
> looked black frock-coats flitted and darted by, singly and
> in clusters, as flies dart over a white, gleaming loaf of
> refined sugar in the summer season, on a sultry July
> day, as an aged housekeeper standing at an open
> window cleaves and divides the loaf into glittering,
> irregular lumps.... (p. 7)

We are perhaps only an amusing half-step away from epic, for Virgil compares Dido's busy Carthaginians to bees when Aeneas first sees them (*Aeneid* 1.430–36), and in the opening scene of *War and Peace* Tolstoy will similarly capture the essence of Anna Scherer's soirée by the simile of a clockwork. Here, ominously, the squinting Chichikov and flitting frock-coats almost become insects before the simile begins, while the insects turn strangely human. To continue:

> all the children, having flocked together, are looking on,
> curiously watching the movements of her roughened
> hands as they lift up the maul, while the aerial
> squadrons of flies, held up by the buoyant air, fly in
> boldly, as if they owned the whole place and, taking
> advantage of the crone's purblindness and of the sun that
> bothers her eyes, bestrew the dainty morsels, in some
> places singly, in others in thick clusters. (p. 7)

Following the best Homeric practice, this simile has developed its own wayward story, and the physical point of comparison (the swarming of the groups) remains clear. But another group, the children, behave like the flies and also bear comparison to the socialites. The comparison becomes confusingly

triangular. The crone's momentary blindness parallels Chichikov's. Are these somehow his impressions? With a curious
mirroring, the flies to whom the socialites are likened themselves
are compared to yet other human beings ("squadrons").

> Sated with the riches of summer, which spreads
> delectable repasts at every step even without such
> windfalls as this, they have flown in not at all in order
> to eat but merely to show themselves, to promenade to
> and fro over the mound of sugar, to rub either their
> hind- or their forelegs against each other, or scratch with
> them under their gossamer wings, or, having stretched
> out their forelegs, rub them over their heads, and then
> once more to turn around and fly away, and once more
> come flying back with new harassing squadrons. (p. 7)

Further precision now ruptures the network of similarities:
flies do not merely promenade, especially on sugar; even the
most muscoid socialites do not rub their legs on their heads. In
the traditional epic simile, the realms of men and of animals
define and reveal each other by discrete resemblances within
larger dissimilarity. Here the two realms, by interpenetrating
and confusing each other, lead us into the realm of the mock-
heroic, and perhaps somewhat beyond. The socialites are not
entirely diminished by the comparison to the flies, because the
flies themselves begin to acquire human and even heroic purpose.
The universe of the simile does have a thriving vitality that this
tiresome provincial ball utterly lacks, for that universe is not
just alive, but growing into a self-sustaining microcosm into
which the reader might happily see the narrative escape. What
interest the comparison confers on the ball is fleeting. More
importantly, it serves to convey the mad, boundary-shattering
energy of the narrator's imagination and his capacity to animate
this moribund landscape by failing to report on it, dull and
predictable as it is, with any steady competence. Every simile
provided to mirror the object at hand tempts the narrator to

step through the looking glass. In other words, what the simile chiefly tells us is that the one interesting person at the ball is the narrator himself, and we do not know to what degree he is or is not Chichikov. Even here one can begin to wonder how long this conspicuous but unidentified voice can confine his wayward imagination to the too easy job of deflating the puny present through evocations of lost heroic grandeur, or of replicating the now quaint heroic forms that once celebrated it.

Mock heroic also relies on the equal and opposite trick of aggrandizing the trivial. We have already seen a simile that makes a Zeus of a bureaucrat. The narrator, apparently bored with his ordinary subject matter, habitually interjects livelier narrative possibilities, and these comparisons, like the similes, have the potential to animate themselves into vignettes. Rather than delineate Nozdrev's fulminations, the narrator compares him to some desperate lieutenant rabidly urging his troops to suicide in battle (p. 74). Instead of dwelling on Korobochka's squalid life, he trades up to the better grade of squalor of Petersburg socialites (pp. 47–48). Partly, N—— is being diminished by comparison to a larger world, partly, by comparison to the expansiveness of the narrator's imagination, erupting from within.

A final example of this device will locate it within the larger pattern of Gogol's texts: when a blonde maiden glides past our hero's coach, the narrator evokes the stunned response of some hypothetical twenty-year-old before dutifully detailing the middle-aged Chichikov's verbose and misogynistic reaction (pp. 78–79). This is our first glimpse of the angelic type who later, as Ulinka, will play the Beatrice/Annunziata role in the uncompleted Part Two—yet another embodiment of that "sublime beauty" that will commence Gogol's survey of the world in *Selected Passages* (chapter 2: "Woman in the World"). Within the pattern of recurrence of such figures, Chichikov's cold reaction here signifies that his preoccupation with externals still blinds him to the emotional and imaginative forces that might be unleashed by this vision. The narrator, however, describes a reaction identical to that which ends "Rome," with the hypothetical twenty-year-old observer "grown oblivious of self, and of his work, and of the world, and of all the things that there are in the world." Even in this digression we are still in the heroic world, though much decayed, of works and deeds and external movement. In this world—as with Helen, Dido, and the fatal Polish beauty of "Taras Bulba"—one should steer clear of sirens. The narrator, however, is more inclined to linger.

Among the squirming bits of life in this comic first half of the narrative, the movement is all mutation, not development, so that much of the humor lies in eternal, mechanical repetition. Chichikov does not evolve in Part One and does not grow into any of the types of heroism that he, at moments, promises to embody. He is not finally an antihero, nor one of the pygmy heroes of mock epic, nor one of the dreamy cousins of heroes who look on from the pastoral pleasance. In his failure to develop, he ends up representing a featureless ordinariness: neither young nor old, rich nor poor, handsome nor repulsive, bright nor dull, loud nor reticent. Indeed, as Gogol characterizes him by elimination in the opening paragraph, we have the distinct impression of our hero's arriving at the equally featureless town of N—— in an empty carriage. Along with his sundry valises and parcels, he seems not to have brought a personality. Neither learning nor changing, he seems content with the fitful progress of his swindle. The various episodes show facets of his character reflected in the various landowners,[31] as they could do equally well in any other order. Though ostensibly describing the grubby "now," the narrator can stitch together the various chapters, like the episodes of "Taras Bulba," as freely as a bard arranges his lays, since the stasis of the subject matter seems to leave it *in illo tempore*, in myth's endless cycles of lost time.

Yet for all the narrator's professed contentment with this stasis and inconsequence, he hides his own sweeping ambitions less and less successfully. His intrusions begin to reveal his impatience with a story that in its eternal circles is failing to accommodate his sense of calling. His emergence into the text makes the latter half almost a reversal of what precedes, even as the same characters file past again to expose Chichikov rather than to collude with him. Digressions still establish scale in the epic manner, but now they are less often similes than autobiographical reflections that advertise narrative subjectivity as clearly as the similes (falteringly) attest bardic distance. Imperceptibly, the surrounding universe changes character: the heroic age winding relentlessly down to vulgarity seems more and more like the coiled spring of Rus' (or at least of the narrator) ready to spring forward. Though we have not departed N—— as the dead and deadening center of a turning universe, Gogol has shifted the epic coordinates on us.

An unsuspected virtue of the middleness of the setting, *nel mezzo del cammin di nostra vita*—the middle-aged Chichikov of moderate gifts and medium rank as he visits the midpoint between Petersburg and Moscow—is that the author can unobtrusively change his mind about what this is the middle *of.* As was noted in chapter 1, the middle distance functions variously in mock heroic and the pastoral. Here we might add Christian parables of Everyman. In the beginning of the narrative, as in *Mirgorod*, a grander age lies beyond, for the current generation lies halfway between their heroic ancestors and the animals to which the author so often compares them. By the end, however, it is the future of Rus' that overshadows the open plain—now less a wasteland than an empty stage awaiting the drama, a desert for the Chosen People to wander, a canvas empty enough to accommodate the narrator's national (or is it personal?) self-portrait. One may attach what meanings one will to these closing vistas, for what matters is no longer the place but the movement through it. The inconsequent "somewhere" of N—— becomes an everywhere by virtue of the narrator's capacity to conceive hopes for it, while the tarnished "ordinary" in his subject matter grows into the instructively "typical," and provincial nonentities become normative Russians. Void is reperceived as freedom. The accommodating mediocrity of N—— thereby allows a shift of project from forging deeds for serfs to forging the consciousness of the race. The very barrenness of the topography allows it to be transformed into the inner landscape of the soul, where time is not cyclical but developmental and progressive. And the narrator, who initially created this world only to join us in mocking it, finds himself trapped within it yet enabled to take us with him as he makes, or promises, his escape.

How this reorientation occurs is worth noting in detail. The sixth chapter brings the narrative to the midpoint of the eleven as the landowner Pliushkin brings Pushkin's anecdote to an end—and can the names be coincidental? As the full and final embodiment of death-in-life, the miser Pliushkin concludes the novel's opening movement, the picaresque tale of descent through the rogues' gallery. Pliushkin presents a Dantesque vision of the *privatio boni* taken to an icy extreme.[32] He will be the single landowner not to show up at Chichikov's trial, where the president of the court inquires: "Is he still leading his frozen existence?" (p. 127)[33] Yet by its very placement, this low moment invokes a lofty heritage. For Chichikov's descent into the lifeless underworld falls at the same point as Aeneas's (in the sixth book of the *Aeneid*'s twelve). And even before this nadir is reached, the voice of the narrator begins liberating itself for higher strains. Up through chapter 5, the narrative has advanced steadily past the chapter beginnings without other flourishes of prelude or peroration. The end of chapter 5, however, takes a maximally incongruous moment (a muzhik's deleted expletive describing Pliushkin) as an occasion for celebrating Mother Russia: "The Russian people have a puissant way of expressing themselves!" (p. 94). The topic is suitably epic: the bestowing of epithets, their ineradicability, and, above all, their quintessential Russianness:

> That which is aptly uttered is tantamount to that which
> is written: there's no rooting it out, though you were to
> use an ax. And how very apt, of a certainty, is that
> which has come out of the very core of Russia, where
> there is no German, nor French, nor Finnish, nor any
> other sort of tribe, but the purest virgin gold, the living
> and lively Russian wit, that is never at a loss for a word,
> that doesn't brood over it, like a setting hen, but comes
> spang out with it, like a passport to be carried through
> all eternity, and there's no use your adding on later what
> sort of nose or lips you have: you are drawn, at a stroke,
> from head to foot!

The passage embodies the Russian wit that it celebrates by
mixing the imagery associated with violence (ax), domesticity
(mother hen), and diplomacy (passport)—all seen epically sub
specie aeternitatis. The Gogolian perversity of celebrating the
all-creating Russian Word in the context of a censored epithet
recapitulates the mock-heroic gestures of the title page as it
thwarts the censors.

To an equal and opposite extent, the creating Word also
evokes serious Christian reflections, which Gogol addresses with
typically bizarre analogies and apparent enthusiasm in the chapter's final paragraph. As are the multitudes of churches in
Russia, so are the numberless peoples of the earth. And each
people has its word: the Englishman's, wise; the Frenchman's,
flashy; the German's, ponderous: "But there is never a word
which can be so sweeping, so boisterous, which would burst out
so, from out of the very heart, which would seethe so and quiver
and flutter so much like a living thing, as an aptly uttered
Russian word!" This first celebration calls to mind, of course,
the apostrophe of Russia in the troika scene that will end Part
One. Both passages treat the Russian landscape as set apart
from and above anything European, and lexically the passages
coincide surprisingly. In both we find the words *Rus'* (Rus',
Russia); *narod* (nation); *zemlya* (land); *vsyakii* (every); *sila*

(strength); *Bog* (God); *boiko* (lively, adroitly). Perhaps also not coincidentally, chapter 5 had earlier introduced the fixtures of the final scene: "again there remained only the road, the light carriage, the troika of horses familiar to the reader, Seliphan, Chichikov, and the smooth and empty expanse of the surrounding fields" (p. 78). The Russian word giving birth to itself here, near the midpoint of Part One, announces a concept of literary autogenesis which, as we shall see, looms large in Gogol's later writing. It seems an almost inevitable gesture for a writer intent on launching a national tradition. Can it be coincidental that it comes just before the adieu to Pushkin/Pliushkin in chapter 6?

The first sign of a new narrative dimension is the narrator's emergence to self-consciousness rather than his earlier random blurting into the text. This emergent voice is a creation out of the void, even as the Russian word proclaims itself out of a deletion. For the narrative voice announces itself as stillborn, brooding over the sensations of youth now lost to it. That is, the bard of Chichikov's odyssey presents himself as a bored and incurious traveler: "Now I drive up apathetically to every unfamiliar village and look apathetically at its vulgar appearance; to my time-chilled gaze things seem bleak, and I am not amused, and that which in former years would have aroused an animated expression, laughter, and unceasing speeches, glides past me now and an impassive silence do my expressionless lips preserve. Oh, my youth! Oh, my fresh vigor" (p. 96). With characteristic paradox, the new bardic voice intrudes to announce itself with an apologia for its silence! The next words alert us to another curiosity that will persist: the narrator can speak for himself only when his hero is wool-gathering or sleeping. Chichikov had been inwardly chuckling over the deleted epithet, so it turns out that the narrator has only articulated what Chichikov was thinking. After the narrator makes his revelations, Chichikov wakes up. They exist in a reciprocity never quite explained to us, as if two sides of one personality.

The blurrings of identity continue. It is Pliushkin, not
Chichikov, who more extremely suffers the spiritual death that
the narrator diagnoses for himself with fearful hyperbole. Like
all of the landowners, Pliushkin is a mirror for Chichikov, but
the salient resemblance is to the narrator. Just as it is age that
has eroded the latter's soul, so Pliushkin presents above all "the
frigid, insensate features of inhuman old age" (p. 111). As if to
point the moral for Chichikov and the narrator as travelers,
Pliushkin's spiritual death is figured in the allegory of life as
journey:

> Take along with you, then, on setting out upon your
> way, as you emerge from the gentle years of youth into
> stern, coarsening manhood, take along with you all the
> humane impulses, abandon them not on the road; you
> will never retrieve them after! Sinister, fearsome is the
> old age that will come upon you farther along the way,
> and it never releases aught nor ever aught returns!
> (p. 111)

Yet the parallel of the narrator with Pliushkin suggests even
more by the way that it inevitably breaks down. Frozen in place,
Pliushkin disappears from the tale; the narrator is just warming
up. His profession of silence contradicts itself in the very act
of being spoken. His blocked channels of perception are belied
by the existence of the vivid tale that he conveys to us. Far
from being static and moribund, he emerges into the text to
become the most changeable, elusive, and lively figure in it.
The narrator has, to be sure, classed himself among the dead
souls who are his subjects, as well as with the traveler who is
his hero. Yet by the logic of the self-creating word, this voice
seems able to come to life by the very act of diagnosing its own
death. In the beginning was the Word. And the Word said, "I
am dead," and, lo, there was life. Such seems the destiny of
the Russian Word.

For all the novelty and insouciance of this self-christening,
it coincides with other important moments of literary emergence.

The image of the journey recalls that the Russian novel had to this point launched itself quite literally into various journeys: *Eugene Onegin* commences with the hero's racing off to his uncle's deathbed and, in several unfinished chapters (usually placed after the conclusion of the work), recounts the disenchanted and directionless dandy's trip to Odessa and other points south. *A Hero of Our Time* opens with the narrator's account of his travels, shortly to focus on Pechorin himself, "the military man on the move," whose "road pass" represents a passport for excursions inside the psyche, a reason for the roving, questioning search to come. Further back, epic itself in its canonical Virgilian form radiates out from the wandering of Aeneas and the Trojans, as of Odysseus before them. Most suggestively, the allegorical overlay of Chichikov's journey as it figures the narrator's journeys (both in Russia and in writing) as they, in turn, figure the journey of life itself (as the above reflections of Pliushkin make explicit) calls to mind the distinctive allegories of Dante-poet, Dante-pilgrim, and the journey of this life. Lest the parallel escape the reader, Gogol notes of the collegiate registrar that he "served our friends even as Virgil on a time had served Dante" (p. 126). As the narrative voice creates itself from the void, it recalls *The Divine Comedy*'s vision of the new creating consciousness speaking itself into existence from the world of the dead.[34] Gogol will leave the moral allegory quite unconcealed by the end: "What twisted, god-forsaken, narrow, impassable by-paths that have diverted it far from the goal has not mankind chosen in its strivings to attain the eternal truth, when spreading right before it was an open way, like to a path that leads to a great fane, meant for a king's mansions" (p. 198)—a far remove from the nonreligious, almost existential point of view in the novels of Pushkin and Lermontov.

That Pliushkin should serve as the pivot for this transformation of plot and narrative style is something of a curiosity. Transparent to all and harmful chiefly to himself, he makes the least likely candidate for villain. Unlike the other landowners, he affects subsequent events only by his absence. Of the series, he is the most inert. So is Satan frozen into ice at the bottom of Dante's Inferno; he, too, without moving can support a large narrative shift. As noted above, already Homer and Virgil had assigned to the strengthless dead pivotal roles—indeed, right in the middle of the *Odyssey* and *Aeneid*—in the unfolding destinies of those who still live and act. To understand the structural shift in *Dead Souls* here at the middle we must look more closely at how Pliushkin epitomizes evil despite his self-limiting and harmless obsessiveness: he manifestly lacks the vivacity and mystery of wickedness, as well as its seductiveness. He comes closer to the medieval vision of the Devil as an ass. Within the featureless geography of *Dead Souls* he forms the middle point (narratively and morally) of a world paralyzed by "middleness," and therefore the extreme point of a world dangerously lacking in extremes. He exists, that is, in a mode of inert undifferentiation, chaos, the primal soup that preexists the discriminating fiats of the creating Word that set light and dark, land and sea apart from one another. His essence lies in the lack of essence, the deadening blurring of categories.

Pliushkin presents perceptual problems not hitherto encountered. Chichikov initially mistakes the master of this estate for a woman and a servant—naturally enough since Pliushkin, rich as he is, plays the beggar. For him, to administer is to imprison, with himself also as prisoner. Only here among Chichikov's purchases of souls do living runaways get mixed up with the dead serfs. This living embodiment of evil as moral absence is reprised in the registrar who figures in Chichikov's biography: "There was just nothing at all in him, either of wickedness or of goodness, and there was a manifestation of something fearful in this absence of everything" (p. 216). Chichikov's first view of Pliushkin's estate, luxury overlaid with squalor, testifies to the promiscuous erosion even of the categories of art and nature, man and what is not man:

Some of these aspens had branches broken but not
completely severed, which dangled, their leaves all
withered. In short, everything was as beautiful as
neither Nature alone nor art alone can conceive, but
only as when they come together, when over the labor of
man, often heaped up without any sense, Nature will
run her conclusive burin, will lighten the heavy masses,
will do away with the coarsely palpable regularity and
the beggar's rents, through which the unconcealed,
naked plan peers through, and bestow a wondrous
warmth to everything that had been created amid the
frigidity of a measured purity and tidiness. (p. 98)

The long surrounding description of the decay and disorder of
"this extinct place" parodies the encomium of the perfecting
hand of time and moss among the ruins of "Rome." Like the
Roman prince, Chichikov has become an observer, and he is
being seduced by a garden suited to the perversity of his soul—
not presided over by Calypso or Alcina, but a miser; not a
Bower of Bliss, but the living death of uncommitted undifferentiation, a remaking of the Wood of the Suicides in *Inferno*
13.[35] Art and nature join together not to perfect one another
but to cancel each other out and produce a warmth that is the
warmth of rot.

Pliushkin therefore carries the confusions and blurred
boundaries of this irredeemably ordinary land to an extreme,
indeed to a point where he dislodges the narrator from his
continuing search for the typical and the Russian to a diagnosis
that Pliushkin can be the exception that proves the rule: "It
must be said that one encounters such a phenomenon but rarely
in Russia, where all things love to open up rather than to shrivel
into a ball like a hedgehog" (p. 104).[36] As the final erosion of
boundary and order, Pliushkin, this void, this "rent on the cloak
of humanity" (p. 104), serves to offer standards for judging the
rest. By comparison, Nozdrev's compulsive lies, which similarly
obliterate distinction, retrospectively take on a certain vivacity,

as for example in the delicious absurdity of marching the hungry
Chichikov up to a boundary stone that divides what Nozdrev
owns from (how can he resist the claim?) what he also owns
on the other side (p. 62). That kind of imaginative confusing
of things seems benign compared to the killing literalism of
Pliushkin, who, very like a writer, shapes his private world into
a microcosm but ends up with trash heaps rather than fictions
because he collects things instead of words. As an odious embodiment of a kind of literalism, Pliushkin marks the point
beyond which the reader can no longer read literally and must
open up to the allegories that now begin to spin themselves out
from the text.

Reading habits often mark the man in this narrative: Chichikov and Petrushka read without concern for content (the
one, ripped-down posters; the other, any book that falls into
his hands); Nozdrev has a study in which he keeps only guns.
Pliushkin collects paper, but only for the purpose of keeping it
blank. Ominously, he is the landowner most instantly in accord
with Chichikov's scheme, and indeed even expands it to include
runaways. The end of chapter 6 suggests that, as can happen
in underworld journeys, Chichikov has come away from this
visit infected with the disordering perspective that robbed
Pliushkin of life. In a world where moral pathology centers on
mediocrity and undifferentiation, the heart of darkness is twi-
light: "It was already dusk when they [Chichikov and Seliphan]
drove up to town. Light and shadow had become thoroughly
intermingled and, it seemed, all objects had also become intermingled among themselves" (p. 114). In the remainder of Part
One, Chichikov, as increasingly fantastic tales gather around
him, will not know whether the townspeople are mad or he is
mad, or perhaps stuck in a nightmare. In escaping Pliushkin's
estate, Chichikov does not escape the moral vacuum that it
represents.

As Fanger[37] notes, it is with Pliushkin that time enters the
narrative. As in other ways, the old miser dispatches his struc-

tural role rather paradoxically, for the new temporal dynamic in the narrative is inspired by this most static of the characters, the one decisively eroded beyond all change. His character is epitomized by the broken pocket-watch that he contemplates giving to Chichikov (and does not). But broken timepieces imply the existence of those that still work, just as Pliushkin does the existence of people still alive. The narrative to follow will proceed against the background of a ticking clock, a doom waiting to descend on Chichikov (and possibly the narrator), as well as a heightened sense of history—a reminder that these are the years after 1812 and perhaps, therefore, a moment for Russia to be going somewhere. The very lifelessness of Pliushkin calls into question the life that made him thus; he alone among the landowners has a biography. As we have seen, the narrator introduces this episode by his own autobiographical reflections. Here begins the movement that will culminate in Chichikov's biography at the end of Part One, as well as the narrator's reflections, following the Public Prosecutor's death, on the proper relationship among the generations of human beings, that is, on the claims of tradition. In all, the visit to Pliushkin, as underworld visitations are wont to do, has worked dialectically: the step out of time enables progress; departing the bounds of human morality creates terms for discrimination. This structural motif repeats itself at the end of Part One, when Chichikov's final liberation follows from an encounter with the Public Prosecutor's funeral cortege. As Seliphan notes, "That's a good thing, though, meeting this funeral; they say meeting a dead man is an omen of good luck" (p. 207).

Among the discriminations precipitated by Pliushkin's moral inertness is that of the narrator from his narrative. He becomes sufficiently aware of his own consciousness and problems (the audience, eternally the audience) that he can discuss them separately from the narrative, which, not coincidentally, at this crucial point begins to complicate and advance itself rather than just accreting vignettes. As noted above, the nar-

rator's descent into the text generates vertical dimensions, relations between creator and created, that compound the allegorical meanings of the text. From the first, one has been able
to read literally and with amusement. Yet now, thinking back
over the various landowners, one begins to sense that these
comic "types" may also serve a more profound moral allegory—
not, to be sure, of murderers, traitors, and simonists, but of
those who are neither hot nor cold. As Marianne Shapiro points
out, the landowners, with their lack of moral commitment, could
all fit comfortably into Dante's Limbo.[38] That suspended, excluded state of the moral neutrals—neither in Hell nor quite
out of it—becomes another way of conceiving the middleness
and mediocrity out of which Gogol has built N——. And beyond
this allegory, confirmed by the narrator's discussion of the symbolism of the road, comes a third level (to use Dante's schema),
the moral, as the narrator introduces himself with his preoccupations about the well-being of his soul and of the text that
expresses it.

This narrator, as we shall see, will stand in a variety of
relationships with the protagonist: sometimes coextensive with
his consciousness, sometimes as a foil, sometimes entirely separate. Doubtless this relationship is kept problematic not only
for the purposes of comedy but because it implies so much about
the most dangerous relationship of all, that of the narrator to
Gogol himself. In other words, an analogy inevitably suggests
itself between the authorial "voice" in the text (narrator : Chichikov) and the author himself (Gogol : narrator). By
calling his pilgrim "Dante," Dante sets up an identity among
protagonist, narrator, and author. By contrast, Gogol prevents
Chichikov from seeming simply a projection of the narrator's
own identity and thereby keeps the narrator from seeming simply
a hypostasis of himself, that is, some unfictionalized record of
his own voice. By the same token, the sporadic interpenetration
of the consciousnesses of Chichikov and the narrator implicates

Gogol himself, again fragmentarily but tantalizingly, in his nervous narrator.

The blurring of allegory prepares for a climactic evasion, for it is in the troika scene that we are left with no way of telling whether this is a vision or a joke. The narrator has an expansive sense of Russian destiny. Chichikov has none, so far as we know. What, then, of Gogol? Does he write more of himself into his patriotic, overwrought narrator or his cynical protagonist? He leaves us with the sense that he, personally, may have the vision or lack it or sustain both propositions by the ironic sense that all visions are jokes, as the creating Russian Word, born of its own deletion, might lead us to expect. As noted at the outset, this irony is a complex development from the essentially mock-heroic humor of the opening narrative, for it directly assaults the basis of that irony—namely, the ability of author and audience to stand securely superior to what is being described. The status of the author and, as we shall see, of the audience, has become acutely problematic, and the ironies of the creating, uncreating Russian Word do not generate mocking distance from the text but implosion, a sense of unleashed energies that are at once redemptive and nihilistic, generative and self-canceling, saccharine and sacrificial, and that thereby witness to the impossibility of reducing the Russian spirit to any single philosophical, religious, or political principle.

The plot of *Dead Souls* does not so much resolve and seal itself off as shift its coordinates to another temporal dimension, another pattern of narration, within which narrative resolution would have no meaning, a dimension with no more closure than the evanescent "now" of experienced time. The plot, insignificant as the narrator claims it is, means little. The shift means everything, and it is also the watershed in Gogol's career. Like the *Mirgorod* cycle (and every Greek tragedy), the narrative is framed by entrances and exits: Chichikov comes to town; Chichikov leaves town. The bachelor carriage is the same; the servants are the same; and Chichikov thinks he is the same.

But the very fact that we know this unremarkable last item makes all the difference, for in the interval we have crawled inside Chichikov's head. The carriage is the same; the road is the same; it is the audience that is not the same.

Through its first half, *Dead Souls* proceeds so episodically that, like *Mirgorod*, it could as well be separate tales. As the link element, the hollow Chichikov could just as well be given a variety of names and identities. In fact he is, when his victims variously describe him as a counterfeiter, a spy, Napoleon, the abductor of the Governor's daughter, or Kopeikin. They themselves end with no strong sense of all having been in the same story; indeed, they end up spinning out stories (Nozdrev's fantasies, the Postmaster's tale of Captain Kopeikin) in the vignette style of the first six chapters—aggrandized, psychologically flat, pointless. They are doing what the narrator used to do, while he has moved on to something else. For the great advance in Gogol's artistry shows itself in the wake of Pliushkin, as the parts cohere and interact ever more closely into a single action. Our distracted narrator still afflicts us with gaps and discontinuities, but now they are less the interstices between vignettes strung out in a row (Chichikov's various visits) than leaps to different levels of a concerted action, levels that communicate with one another along some unexplained but constantly rattling chain of being. Initially, narrator and audience sat in Olympian amusement over the pomps and alarums of this pygmy village, while the stasis of the characters and simple linking of one episode to another evoked the sense of cyclic, nonprogressive time found in "Taras Bulba" and classical epic, a harmlessly remote "then." In the last six chapters, however, autobiography and biography bring instead a notion of time as experienced from within—that is, as developmental, linear, and subsumed into the continuing "now." This is the temporal continuum of "Rome" as it follows in the wake of the grand scheme bequeathed to epic by Dante, that is, the vision of pilgrimages not sealed off *in illo tempore* but leading ultimately to the writer

and the reader, the infinitely deferred closure of a lost, yet
unlosable and still beckoning paradise. The bard buys that
dream at the price of his anonymity and in descending from
his perch confers new vertical dimensions on his creation, dimensions that need not be solemn to be real.

So it is that our slightly haunted narrator loses his detachment from the text, as episodes mesh into orchestrated movements—he senses conspiracy—that attest to a narrator strongly
in control of, though also strongly controlled by, his text. As
the narrator discloses his own inner life, he confers such a
dimension upon his characters. He even anticipates it in his
audience, thereby eroding the anonymity and ironic distance
with which he began the tale. It was initially the sophisticated
narrator who tarted up the grubby tale with epic flourishes for
the delectation of his sophisticated audience. But by the end it
is the Postmaster and Nozdrev who have expropriated the overblown style. The tale of the brigand Kopeikin comes to us with
a filigree of allusions to Scheherazade, Semiramis, Lethe, "a
whole epic, in a sort of way," claims the Postmaster (p. 185).
And it is no more the narrator's sophisticated audience but the
erstwhile pygmies of N—— who, with vast credit to their own
intelligence, do the dismissing. That is, the initial mock-heroic
ironies of *Dead Souls*, the interaction of narrator and audience,
have been absorbed into the text itself, so that we see a reflection—crude, but unmistakable—of the skeptical and self-
congratulatory audience that we have lately been.

In the Christian confessional mode of epic, it is of course
the writer's own spiritual development that is ultimately called
to account. In contrast to the narrative freedom, almost ran-
domness, of the first half, after Pliushkin there comes an in-
creasing feeling of things *following*:[39] as the townspeople close
in on Chichikov and as the narrator senses his audience closing
in on him, claustrophobia and causation develop in tandem, so
that increasingly one thing narratively has to follow upon another. Herein lurks the seamless vision of "Rome" or of the

Paradiso turned into nightmare. The deadening obsession with acquisition that in the first half freezes the characters into stasis now gives way to an eruptive and illimitable growth of consciousness, which closes in on narrator and protagonist as it threatens almost literally to waken the dead, or the audience.

The narrator and protagonist at moments coincide to such a degree that, for example, when Chichikov risks contamination by Pliushkin, it is the narrator who feels impelled to profess his own immunity to the epidemic loss of perspective, as he does at the beginning of the next chapter. Here begins the self-defense that evolves throughout the rest of the narrative by means of protracted reflection on the writer's lot figured in terms of a journey. Indeed, it is the integrating image of the journey, the road rather than the stops along it, that signals the narrative shift toward continuity. The narrator's celebration of his vocation, mixed with self-mockery and self-defense, may parallel those epic writers (for example, Apollonius Rhodius, Virgil [i.e., *Aen.* 7.37–45], and Milton) who commence the latter halves of their works with new invocations of the Muses. Indeed, the narrator admits to the help of a similar "wondrous power" (p. 117), if not quite the traditional sisterhood, in composing his tale. To be sure, his intent is not to espouse but to decline the calling to heroic song. The *recusatio* of the high style, the solemn refusal of the epic vocation, is a fixture of classical rhetoric, a way of evading the pretensions of patrons. Yet within the allegories generated by the Christian, spiritual reading of such acts, *recusatio* can function nobly as renunciation; self-abasement becomes self-fulfilment; the ordinary becomes the redemptively humble; what in secular terms is the lower calling becomes a spiritually true vocation.

A single statement, therefore, can be both an abashed apology for foregone heroics and a triumphant proclamation of spiritual allegory in the text:

> happy the writer who has picked out only the few
> exceptions from the great slough of everyday figures

revolving around him; the writer who has not changed
even once the lofty strain of his lyre, has never
descended from his aerie to his poor, insignificant
brethren, and who, without touching the common earth,
has devoted himself wholly to his images and forms, far
removed from that earth and enlarged to heroic size. . . .

   But not such is the lot and different is the fate of
the writer who has dared to bring out all the things that
are before man's eyes at every minute, yet which his
unheeding eyes see not—all that fearsome, overwhelming
slimy morass of minutiae that have bogged down our
life, all that lurks deep within the cold, broken,
workaday characters with which our earthly path, at
times woeful and dreary, swarms. (p. 116)

On one, more literal level, the narrator, in an apologia that is
as old as Aristophanes, begs only that we not confuse him with
his ignoble subject matter or, perhaps more gravely, suspect that
he shares the fatal lack of discrimination that has reduced
Pliushkin from man to thing and to which Chichikov shows
himself susceptible. After the countless proemia in which some
poet claims to sing a higher strain (*paulo maiora canamus*),
here the writer openly sings of his vocation to the low road.
However, by a more allegorical and Christian reading, the absorption with "poor, insignificant brethren" is not frailty but
evangelism, and the true Muses are evoked not on the slopes
of Helicon but in the confessional.

   The narrator has begun Pliushkin's chapter with a confession that he suffers the same erosion of sensitivity by time
already infecting Chichikov (who saw nothing in the lovely
blonde but a potential dowry) and which has entirely robbed
Pliushkin of human emotion. The account of Pliushkin is sufficiently appalling that to balance the personal confession introducing it (at the beginning of chapter 6) there needs to be
literary self-defense to conclude and isolate it. And the narrator
does insist on the point that this low road is where life actually

thrives and swarms—a truth deducible already from the vivacious flies and dull socialites of the opening soirée, but now
affirmed in the mode of authorial self-reflection rather than epic
simile. Author and audience looked down mockingly on the flies
on that sugarloaf; increasingly, they will find themselves squirming there below.

Luckily, before the narrator gets lost entirely in his brooding
self-reflections, he lets Chichikov wake up: "Let us plunge
suddenly and head first into life, with all its inaudible blather
and jingle-bells, and see what Chichikov is up to" (p. 117).
Thus the narrative of the second part of the novel begins with
the image of plunging ahead with which it will end, though
here it is the narrator and readers who do the plunging, as later
Chichikov will do when we have reached our stopping point.
Awakening proves to be the dominant theme of the rest of Part
One, as Chichikov quite unintentionally stirs the townspeople
first into frenzied admiration and then into rampaging speculation about his identity and purposes. Their lackluster sameness
of values and habits gives way to the brilliant particularity of
their convictions about the man, as these fantasies variously
derive from fear, jealousy, desire, and a total lack of proportion.
The gray, faceless populace now begins to differentiate itself:
men and women harbor quite diverse suspicions about the mysterious stranger, as do servants and masters. As we have noted,
the range of their accounts, from the grotesque and almost
folkloric to the heroic (Chichikov is Napoleon) reflects what has
been the narrator's own range of styles. The creating Russian
Word seems to be working its strange magic, if only in the form
of gossip (but the narrator has made no loftier claims for it).
In fact, by the time we come to the Postmaster's tale of Captain
Kopeikin, the villagers would seem to have reached the state
where they themselves could have written the first chapters of
Dead Souls and thereby force the audience, as noted above, to
self-reflection about how they themselves read those chapters.

It is perhaps here in the text that Gogol's ironies reach most deeply into tales within tales and frauds within fictions when the narrator gives us the Postmaster spinning an overblown and underplotted tale of the nonentity Kopeikin (so like the nonentity Chichikov), as he fabricates a heroic, indeed redemptive, identity for himself (and, like Chichikov, carefully gives his victims receipts). Here we see the interaction of author and audience replicated simultaneously at various levels. At the bottom of this vortex of ironic self-reflection we find Gogol's eerie insight into his own potential, virtually a map of his career. For Kopeikin calls to mind that single, multileveled entity Chichikov-narrator-Gogol. However, Kopeikin's progress from pointless wandering to success as a brigand and organizer neatly reverses Chichikov's career in N——, for Chichikov does bring the villagers together—but to his own cost. The narrator (and implicitly Gogol) ends by claiming that galvanizing effect for himself.

It is, however, with Kopeikin's next step that the parallels become compelling, for he leaves Russia and then redeems it by writing letters back to it, to which the czar himself proves receptive—precisely what Gogol was to do with *Selected Passages from Friends*. At the very core of this embedded text, of fictions compounding themselves, we hit on a stratum of fact. The telos of this account of deceitful bureaucrats who turn the innocent Kopeikin himself to brigandage and trickery is the writing of letters to the czar that reveal an important and unacknowledged truth. It was serious business for Gogol to bring the czar into the text, whatever the degree of distance through narrative framing. He does so in the context of the increasingly apparent project of saving Russia. The Postmaster does not know the end of the tale. Having disseminated his great truth, Kopeikin may have returned to Russia and to his earlier fictions by coming back to Russia disguised as Chichikov. Unless the maimed Kopeikin has also grown a leg and an arm, the Postmaster's audience remains unconvinced. But in perhaps

the most framed, distanced, and ironic point in the text, Kopeikin presents a paradigm of fiction turning itself inside out
into truth, a paradigm that generalizes itself to Chichikov and
the narrator and, better than he knew, to Gogol himself, who
was to live out his last years as if plotted from this fiction.

Meanwhile, the narrator, with a bit more deliberation than
Chichikov, has set about waking up his audience, as his earlier
cringing courtesy gives way to exhortation, baiting, and vocif-
erous self-defense—a homiletic function basic to Christian epic
and unknown to classical. Having descended fully into his own
creation to assume a voice and a function, the narrator takes
his prophetic function seriously. His audience, like the citizens
of N——, should come to feel themselves as a group. This
summoning of the reader from obedient passivity is itself a
creation, a calling from nothing into consciousness. And, as the
first lecture on the subject established, the creating Russian
Word can just as well be a servant's curse as anything else.
Basic to the narrator's message is that his readership feel themselves to be Russians and members of their generation, with
responsibilities to those earlier and those yet to come. Like
Chichikov and the narrator, the audience acquires origins and
posterity—indeed, in heightened terms of apocalypse that address it as fully an epic audience:

> The present generation sees everything clearly now; it
> wonders at the delusions and laughs at the lack of
> comprehension of its ancestors, not perceiving that this
> chronicle is written over with heavenly fire, that every
> letter therein is calling out to it, that from every
> direction a piercing forefinger is pointed at it, at it and
> none other than it, the present generation. But the
> present generation laughs and, self-reliantly, proudly
> launches a new succession of delusions, over which its
> descendants will laugh in their turn, even as the present
> generation is laughing now.

> Chichikov was utterly unaware of what was going
> on. As ill-luck would have it, he had contracted a slight
> cold at this time.... (p. 198)

The juxtaposition of the oblivious Chichikov to the now prophetic
narrator indicates how far the two have grown apart, even though
both have come to a point where they confront a mob of critics.
Like the most pessimistic and demonic of the early fictions ("A
Terrible Vengeance" and "The Portrait"), Part One resolves
itself into a day of reckoning, a final moment of exposure. That
moment involves the narrator vis-à-vis his audience as fully as
it does Chichikov before the citizens of N——. Indeed, since
the latter meets his downfall when the townspeople start paying
attention to him instead of his fictions, one wonders if the self-
absorbed and self-proclaiming narrator is not courting the same
disaster.

Chichikov will stumble forward in his eternal present, having learned nothing. The readership, however, no longer has
that option, as the narrator turns the joke on them. Yes, to
plunge from lofty abstractions to Chichikov's head cold is still
amusing. But the long temporal dimension here presented sub
specie aeternitatis changes the mode of the satire and retroactively causes the reader's condescending laughter to ring hollow.
As we have laughed at these vain and dead souls, so will later
men laugh at us—if we even have the luck to receive the kind
of memorial that the citizens of N—— have received in this
text. Whether this chronicle is written over with heavenly fire
or, as the audience may suspect, with provincial fireflies, matters
less than their realization of their own vantage point, both
infinitely distant and subjectively trapped within the fiction
itself. The extrinsic perspective, the long view of epic, forces
the audience to the paradoxical recognition that these figures
are themselves. From this viewpoint, the readers must confront
the prospect that by insisting (as the narrator anticipates we
will) on subjects nobler than these for "epics," we leave ourselves

without the chance of a memorial. Merely raising the issue further ruptures the closure of the narrative, for beyond the time of composition lies the time of reading, which, barring apocalypse, even the audience cannot finally define and limit.

To be sure, the contradictions in which the narrator mires himself only grow as he progresses. The more he insists on a higher consciousness—in morality, in national identity, in a sense of tradition and destiny—the odder seems his commitment to low subject matter. The very essence of the Russianness that he is trying to distill in this epic is a vitality that cannot be captured in writing: "And lifeless will seem beside them [noble Russians] all the virtuous people of other tribes, even as a book is lifeless before the living word!" (p. 210). The spirit animates; the word kills. We are forced by the compounding contradictions before us to read at a higher, allegorical level. No more than for Dante is comedy excluded thereby: if the narrator's highest use, like Chichikov's, is to be a provocateur, to wheedle, abuse, or cheat people into consciousness, then logical consistency would only weigh him down, as ethics would Chichikov (or scrutability would Socrates). The ultimate hero of the piece is neither the protagonist nor the narrator, but Russia—that is, the readership, the completers and creators of the allegorical decipherment that transmutes this *commedia* into an instructive parable. To make either Chichikov or his narrating double estimable or even finally comprehensible would risk the act of erecting a false idol.

The narrator ends his tale with more force than control, more speed than direction, and a question rather than a denouement. The final epiphanic moment in *Dead Souls* may reveal more than the narrator can quite keep reins on. He amplifies Chichikov's current uncertainties into a question of national destiny. The tone may verge on the inflated and mock-heroic, but the question gets asked nonetheless: Whither Russia? The narrator, having thoroughly abused his patient readership and provided no proper resolution for his plot, seems fully as much in flight as Chichikov and, in retrospect, about as trust-worthy. He need not label or explain his final moment. It is sufficient that he return us to the same carriage, same Chichikov, same road, so that we may realize the degree to which we see them now with different eyes.

Suddenly, with these new consciousnesses, the large sur-rounding shell of the "poèma" is not so empty; or, to put the matter differently, a new and nobler reading is placed on the emptiness. The bare landscape presents, finally, no obstacles to the narrator in imposing heroic expectations, if not heroic value, on this fictive universe. For the sense of absence is seen as coinciding with the challenging emptiness and openness of the Russian landscape. A stagnant backwater comes to seem more and more like the void in which a Second Creation can happen. Whereas the society of N—— had proved frustrating to the narrator, complete absence leaves the imagination free. As seen initially in mock-heroic terms, the mediocrity of protagonist and locale stood as an Iron Age degenerated from some Golden Age. With the new set of coordinates, middleness becomes centrality, a midpoint in a new creation, the birth of consciousness—an organizing topic in Christian epic.

As we have seen already in numerous ways, the very notion of an epic journey in pursuit of dead souls brings to mind Dante's infernal descent. As the wellspring of Italian litera-ture, Dante would recommend himself to the project of pro-moting Russian literature to world attention. For Gogol, eter-nally split between memorializing Russia and abandoning it, the figure of Dante would also provide a welcome model of how a national identity might be captured only from exile. How convenient for someone of Gogol's bent that Dante had dem-onstrated how the road to high and redemptive seriousness may begin through irony and satire, through sinking into the filth of human weakness and insignificance! One needs only the barest of plots; a pageant of rogues will carry the narrative. The national life can easily insinuate itself into the delicious descent.

In its character portrayal, as well as in the dynamics of tone and voice, *Dead Souls* derives much from Dante's *Inferno*. As has long been appreciated, both works reveal how the living are really dead, sorted out by their characteristic sins and eternally fixed in the landscape. Chichikov himself, especially in the early chapters, functions largely as a reflection of what goes on around him, a foil for the various types he meets; they, in turn, serve as crystallizations of his own nature. In the *Inferno*, Dante-pilgrim proceeds in much the same way, seeing sides of his own nature reflected in the denizens of the various rings. How the various types perceive Chichikov is as indexical of their real natures as are the devils' misperceptions of Dante-pilgrim. As Fanger[40] notes, each of Chichikov's encounters occurs in a landscape conceived to reflect the character of the proprietor; the rings of Hell are emblematic in the same way. The deformative life-force of the Gogolian landscape, nature perceived as rot and overthrow, in its own modest way often calls to mind the antinature of Dante's Hell. Having surveyed many human failings, both the *Inferno* and *Dead Souls* save betrayal for the end (as Chichikov is turned upon and driven out by his erstwhile friends). Both end with a landscape that is the very embodiment of absence: the featureless Russian plain and the lifeless ice that entombs Satan along with the treacherous threesome of Judas, Brutus, and Cassius. Stasis in the latter case and unbounded freedom in Chichikov's prospects seem equal, though opposite, symbols of the lack of meaningful possibility. Perhaps, also, Gogol's bounding, directionless troika is, on a much reduced scale, an inversion of the Trinity in the way that Judas and company are.

Both narratives conclude with the sense of having hit bottom. As Part One ends, the double sense of a final plunge into the abyss yet also of a redemptive surge recalls the turning point between the *Inferno* and the *Purgatorio*, a terrifying fall downward that pivots at the earth's (and Satan's) center to become an ascent. At the end of Part One, Gogol announces that "there

are still two long parts ahead of us" (p. 232), and the critic
Vyazemsky[41] tells us that he directly regarded this first part of
his proposed trilogy as the equivalent of the *Inferno*. That plunge
seems strangely familiar when we take it, for the nadir was
already indicated firmly enough with Pliushkin in chapter 6,
and in equally Dantesque terms, though without any sense of
release or uplift. Characters in Part Two will keep slipping
downward to despond, and in 1847 *Selected Passages* gave voice,
a bit more autobiographically, to the same sense of having only
just hit bottom. Herein we can see a reason why Gogol's ad-
aptations of Dante remain always large in promise and inchoate.
Though invoking Dante's whole spiritual cycle as a program
for his work, Gogol felt powerfully only certain moments within
it, particularly the final drop to the bottom, which he seemed
constantly to be reexperiencing. *Facilis descensus Averno*. The
way up again proved harder to find.

This chapter began with the double descent of the ironist,
and perhaps now we are in a position to appreciate its source.
The descents of mock heroic—of author and audience together
condescending to the hollow pomposities of the world depicted—
give way in the latter half of *Dead Souls* to the redemptive
descent of the creator into his work, even as the paranoid but
well-meaning, and perhaps genuinely visionary, narrator recapitulates a movement from within the *Inferno*, the movement
from pagan to Christian. Virgil-guide can descend into the pit
largely as a satirist, to see and mock. He can instruct others
but cannot, like a pilgrim, see to his own redemption. We are
particularly aware of his role in the early cantos and in our
own first readings of the text. Further descent and deeper
familiarity with the text draw out the antecedents that will
ultimately be of more importance to Dante-pilgrim: the infernal
visits of Saint Paul and of Christ. Their descents involve a
shouldering of responsibility, ultimately martyrdom, that is simultaneously an awakening. The final ambiguity of both Gogol's

troika (advancing or escaping?) and Dante's satanic trinity (the nadir that is the pivot upward) captures the paradoxical spiritual energies here at work.

Dead Souls, *Part Two*

Gogol, notoriously, spent the rest of his life failing to answer either "Whither Rus'?" or "Whither Gogol?". He labored, rather, to establish that they were the same question. Though Dante-pilgrim is similarly reduced at the end of his infernal descent to a state of helplessness, incrimination, and infantilism, he has a miracle and a guide to rescue and lead him to purgation. Gogol seemed not to have been able to find either. He reversed his promising strategy of going to Rome to reinvent Russia into a disastrous attempt to import Rome to Russia. The sequel did get written—and mostly burned (as the dying Virgil and exiled Ovid had ineffectually directed their epics to be). In 1847 *Selected Passages* appeared to offer a troubled Russia counsel and advice until the Second Coming that the sequel's publication would be. The requisite miracles were prophesied, but Gogol still seemed hard-pressed to suggest a Virgil other than himself.

The surviving fragments of Part Two of *Dead Souls* and Gogol's outlines nevertheless show gropings toward a tale of purgation and redemption. The opening landscape, like that of *Purgatorio*, is of a mountain sloping down to the shore. The first character encountered, the landowner Tentetnikov, shows potential for being saved, though, like the procrastinators of Ante-Purgatory, also a tendency to waste time. Like the penitents of Dante's second canticle, he is "simply a fellow crawling between earth and heaven" (p. 239).[42] His biography boasts figures comparable to those that Dante found redemptive: a Virgil in the charismatic teacher Alexander Petrovich, as well as an unmistakable Beatrice, Ulinka. He is thirty-three, that important year in life when Gogol himself finally released *Dead Souls* and reissued "Taras Bulba" and the very age at which

Christ died, as a later Russian writer, Joseph Brodsky, reminds us, musing on his own advancement to this stage:

> Thirty-three, the age of the Perfect Man, the age of
> Christ...Christ lived for thirty-three years, and all the
> time he was following a script. It was all written, but
> only for the space of thirty-three years. At thirty-three
> only one thing can begin: Resurrection. Christ did not
> escape repetition. You can find this "blasphemy" in
> Kierkegaard. The Resurrection is the repetition of the
> process. All life is in a sense repetition. This is the
> lesson of Christ.[43]

Tentetnikov now directly embodies the conflict between writing and doing, words and the world, that had bothered Gogol all along, though now that conflict increasingly expresses itself in the ancient Christian debate about the merits of faith versus works, the *vita contemplativa* versus the *vita activa*, which figures so largely in the *Purgatorio*.

Apart from the opening, Gogol has not inserted the talkative narrator of Part One. In Part Two, the distance between the characters, on the one hand, and the author and his audience, on the other, has narrowed greatly, so that Gogol may either have had trouble finding space in the narrative for this mediating, confessional, self-advertising voice or may have abandoned it so as to let his characters, especially Tentetnikov, stand in some ambiguous but unmistakable autobiographical relationship to himself. The anomie and paralysis that afflict Tentetnikov when he loses his teacher may reflect something of Gogol's reaction to the loss of Pushkin, who had, after all, suggested the idea of Part One and might now be sorely needed to give direction to the sequel. Stirred variously by the challenges of being a gentleman farmer or Ulinka's suitor, Tentetnikov glimpses redemption in forsaking words for action: "Fate meant me to be the owner of an earthly paradise, a prince, but I conspired to make myself a burrower among dead papers"

(p. 248). At other moments he reverts to the oblivion of writing "a great work on Russia" (p. 252)[44] to save the nation with words when he despairs of doing so with deeds.

The great redemptive Russian book that is taken up and abandoned replicates the admonitory letters attributed to Captain Kopeikin and anticipates what *Selected Passages* will actually attempt. When we get to the core of Tentetnikov's malaise, we find that it is above all a reaction to the spiritual extravagances that conclude Part One. For it is Tentetnikov who inherits the crisis of the bounding troika—momentum without direction—which is implicitly the narrator's, Gogol's, and Russia's. Tentetnikov experiences his crisis in just these terms:

> What did these sobs mean? Did his ailing soul reveal thereby the grievous secret of its ailment—that the exalted inner being which had begun to rise up within him had not succeeded in taking shape and growing strong; that, not having been put to the test in his youth by a struggle against fiascoes, he had not attained to the high ability of rising higher and becoming stronger by overcoming barriers and obstacles; that, having become molten like metal at great heat, the rich reserve of great emotions within him had failed to receive its final tempering; and now, unresilient, his will was impotent; that the extraordinary preceptor had died too prematurely to benefit him, and that there no longer was anybody in the whole world who had the power to raise up anew the forces shaken by eternal vacillations and the impotent will deprived of its resiliency, who could have called out to his soul as an awakening call that heartening word "Onward!" which the Russian thirsts after everywhere, no matter what rung of the ladder he may be standing on, of whatever station, calling, and pursuit he may be? (p. 252)

This passage gives a fair sense of the conceptual evolution of the text thus far. Part One had moved from static vignettes to a sense of biographical and autobiographical time. Here the perspective moves beyond clock time altogether into a nonlinear dimension of spiritual or psychological time. Tentetnikov's (or Gogol's or Russia's) inability to advance results from no current circumstance, no lack of opportunity or resources, but from a developmental failure, the missed chance of being tempered, challenged, and hardened at the right time.

The phrasing of the next paragraph moves beyond the fictional context altogether into a meditation on what has emerged as the central evangelical project of *Dead Souls*: "Where is he, then, who would be able to tell our Russian soul in its native tongue this omnipotent word 'Onward!'—he who, knowing all the forces and abilities and all the profundity of our nature, could with a single thaumaturgic wave of his hand set us streaming toward the exalted life?" (p. 252). Parts of this allegory are stereotypical: this dark moment of despair over the lost preceptor and the resulting life of error leads directly to the emergence of the redemptive Ulinka—a shift from Virgil-guide to Beatrice, from the past to a vital present—for Ulinka is "alive as life itself" (p. 253). One suspects as well a more deeply felt lament for Pushkin at this point, and perhaps a dark sense that his passing is something that Gogol can never over-come, a moment that he will never psychologically grow beyond. The style of the valediction is such as to suggest that it can never quite be finished so as to liberate the author for other concerns—and in this it violates the standard allegories of spir-itual pilgrimage. It is on the basis of their limitations that the ghosts of such parent/guide figures (for example, Virgil's An-chises or Dante's Virgil) can be laid to rest. The lost preceptor here is less limited, less forgivable, and less forgettable. For in passing prematurely he failed to save his pupil from easy success, failed to be there, as it were, to apply the reins.

The narrative provides little explanation of how this cir-cumstance might still afflict Tentetnikov; its applicability to Gogol is evident, and we shall still be hearing it in *Selected*

Passages from Correspondence with Friends. Since Part One as
an exercise in provocation predicated its impact on being rejected
by the audience, its popular success has presumably undermined
its message. A prophet honored in his own country loses credibility, and Gogol in *Selected Passages* will go to considerable
lengths to rescind that honor. One senses that Pushkin cannot
be forgiven or forgotten for failing to limit and restrain the
disconcerting experience of literary success, or perhaps even for
suggesting the good idea that led to that affliction in the first
place, especially when he is not present to suggest another to
redeem the situation.

Whatever the mixture of tribute and defiance directed toward Pushkin amid the necromancy of Part One, it apparently
has neither conjured up nor exorcised his ghost, and he casts
his shadow over Part Two in the way of an unshakable influence,
an unpayable debt. From the outset, the bounding energies of
the troika are felt to be compromised by unresolved issues from
the past. As in "Rome," Gogol falters once the moment comes
to shift the focus to an Annunziata or an Ulinka. This blockage
may result not just from the undeveloped symbolism of the
feminine for Gogol but also from the unresolved business of
cutting loose from fathers and mentors. To the degree that
Selected Passages manages to map out, if not to dramatize,
spiritual progress, it is by positing a stringently patriarchal
world of czars, Hebrew fathers, and male authors into which
women are invited only for the honor of being given advice.

Gogol's outline suggests that Tentetnikov was to make a
final purgatorial leap into the world of affairs through a secret
political society, which would lead to exile in Siberia, where
Ulinka was to follow.[45] In liberating himself from his own words
into redemptive suffering and perhaps finally to earthly paradise, Tentetnikov traces something like the same arc as Dante-
pilgrim, who is held back in Ante-Purgatory by the enchantment
of hearing his own poetry sung by his friend Casella, then

advances through voluntary suffering to the Eden on the mountain top, drawn by Beatrice, as Tentetnikov will be by Ulinka.

When Chichikov rejoins the narrative in chapter 2 he seems little changed. Gradually, however, his picaresque wandering transforms itself into pilgrimage. He experiences his visit to the extraordinary estate of the wonder-working Konstanzhoglo as something of a homecoming, as if "he had come into everything he had desired and had cast aside his wanderer's staff, saying 'Enough!'" (p. 308). In his own terms, he begins to contemplate resurrection: "he determined, right then and there, to acquire with the money he would derive from mortgaging his fantastic souls a country seat that would by no means be fantastic" (p. 310). His desire to escape his own fictions parallels Tentetnikov's flight from his own words; he, too, now dreams of a life-mate.

Apparently some salvation was in the cards for characters like Khlobuev, Pliushkin, and Chichikov himself, if only in the trilogy's final canticle.[46] How they were to be saved is a difficult and apparently unsolved question. The characters of Part Two are at least not static and fixed in their damnation, as the characters of Part One initially are. Collectively, they seem very much like the late-repentant waiting in Dante's Ante-Purgatory, destined for purgation but not yet launched. The "prodigal son" Khlobuev (as Chichikov calls him, p. 323) may represent one of Dante's four categories in Ante-Purgatory, the lethargic. His idleness involves him in depressing situations. "But he was saved by a religious streak that in some strange way existed within him side by side with his shiftless way of life" (p. 323). One way or another God always does provide for him. "Reverently, gratefully, would he acknowledge at such a time the unencompassable mercy of Providence, have a mass of thanksgiving said—and begin his shiftless mode of life all over again" (p. 323). As an antithesis to Khlobuev, Gogol portrays the hyperactive but melancholic Konstanzhoglo, perhaps an incarnation of the fourth group in Ante-Purgatory—the preoccupied, mostly princes, who were too busy running the world to save their own souls; Gogol also sees Konstanzhoglo in royal terms ("like a king on the day of his triumphant coronation," p. 307). In this contrast of the wonder-working Konstanzhoglo to the ineffectual Khlobuev, the preoccupied to the lethargic, lurks the opposition of the *vita activa* and the *vita contemplativa*, a subject for Dante as well, as in Dante-pilgrim's dream of Rachel and Leah (canto 27), though Gogol has wittily reversed their respective fecundity (the contemplative figure, unlike Rachel, has six children; the activist Konstanzhoglo, only one).[47]

In one particular, Part Two does come unmistakably close to Dante's vision of purgation: the pursuit of a redeemed vision of art that can parallel the redeemed vision of man. The axis of metamorphosis is not so much, as in Part One, between the human and the bestial or the dead as it is between nature and art. Indeed, any person who stops moving for an instant risks being turned into a representation. Ulinka enters the narrative as "a living figurine" with "a pure, noble facial outline [that] could not have been found anywhere save perhaps on ancient, small cameos. . . . And if one were to translate her, with all the drapes of the dress that clung to her, into marble, she would have been considered the work of some sculptor of genius" (p. 268). Landscapes take on such detail and animation that they begin to look back, forcing the reader into an active relationship with what they depict, as Gogol elsewhere claimed should be the artist's goal. As he wrote to Annenkov:

> If I were an artist, I would depict a special kind of
> scene. What trees and landscapes are now painted!
> Everything is clear, sorted out, determined by the master
> himself, with the spectator able to follow it quite
> logically. I would bunch the trees all up, confuse the
> branches, throw light where no one would expect it—
> those are the kind of landscapes that need to be
> painted.[48]

Thoughts begin spontaneously to express themselves in pictures: when the enamoured Tentetnikov doodles, pictures of Ulinka

automatically appear on the page. The connections between
things and words still lurk in the background; traveling through
Russia becomes a journey through a "living book" (p. 293).
But now even the mock-heroic touches are translated into visual
terms: "Platon Mikhalych was Achilles and Paris rolled into
one: a graceful build, a painter's ideal in height, fresh vigor—
he combined all these" (p. 282). By the continuing comparison
of the Mount of Purgatory to a cathedral, as well as to objets
d'art like the vivacious bas-reliefs along the way (cantos 10 and
12), Dante likewise posed the question of what kind of art can
embody and instruct about the ideal without itself competing
with and thereby obscuring the Creator's own handiwork. How
can the artist celebrate divine perfection through the materials
of a fallen world? The answer lies in an art that reveals and
deflates its own illusions. As an ironist, Gogol should have been
particularly well suited for such instructive self-contradiction,
but it remains to be seen how much his sense of irony survived
the religious intensities of his final years.

The importance of this issue had emerged already in chapter
1, which begins as if continuing the authorial apologies of the
end of Part One:

> But why depict mankind's poverty, and more
> poverty, and the imperfectibility of our life, digging up
> types from the backwoods, from the god-forsaken nooks
> and crannies of our realm? . . . And so we once more find
> ourselves in the backwoods, once more have we stumbled
> upon a nook. But then, what backwoods and what a
> nook! (p. 237)

There follows one of Gogol's most elaborate landscapes, indeed,
almost heroic in its presentation: "Like the titanic rampart of
some unending fortress, with corner turrets and embrasures,
the mountain heights stretched along windingly for hundreds
upon hundreds of miles" (p. 237). This descriptive tour de force
complexly recalls Gogol's earlier ways of starting and ending

narratives. From the barren, symbolically malleable plain at the end of Part One we have moved to a cluttered landscape, yet the feeling of motion, almost flight, continues as the description focuses from this vast topography into a single manor house. Like Part One, the text begins with an entrance—ours, for here "we stumble upon a nook." The large prospects, stratified into layers of historical symbolism, that concluded "Rome" and "Taras Bulba" are reworked here, even to the detail of the reflecting river. Where we had been brought in as the spectators, it turns out that the scene itself, "tree-tops, roofs, and crosses pointing down," in the river "seemed for all the world to be scrutinizing this wondrous image" (p. 238). From the mirroring image the landscape looks back at itself, and what is seen is itself a point of observation, indeed a better one: "The view was very fine, but the inverted view, from the superstructure in the distance, was still finer." This landscape that is an observer is lulled by a musical silence: "All this was enveloped in imperturbable stillness, which was not disturbed even by the echoes of the ethereal singers, lost in ethereal vastnesses—echoes that barely reached one's ears" (p. 238). A noninvocation of nonexistent Muses? What is announced here programmatically at the start is a tendency to turn the tables on the readers, to present them with a pretty scene that then looks back out at them.

Gogol is always given to such reversals, but they had at the start of Part One chiefly concerned matters of proportion and dignity, as the puny became pompous and great phonies tripped over themselves. Here the confusions between observer and observed, the creator and his artifact, which the intrusion of the narrator brought to Part One are built into the order of nature itself. One of the clearest indices we have for the various characters lies in what they manage to see, or fail to see, in what surrounds them. Of Tentetnikov in his spiritual paralysis we learn that "a view which no visitor could observe with indifference, was to all intents and purposes non-existent for

the very master of that village" (p. 241). When he then seeks
remedy in the *vita activa* without sufficient spiritual grounding
and soon loses interest, his ineffectuality stems from perceptual
problems, confusions of the great and the small, very like those
of the slightly dizzy narrator of Part One: "if the rustic labors
were being carried on near at hand, his eyes would be fixed on
some point as remote as possible; if the work was going on at
a distance, his eyes would seek out objects as near as possible
..." (pp. 250–51). His temporary delusion that his estate is
actually "an earthly paradise" delays his true pursuit of same.
And Chichikov himself must be warned off his own newfound
aesthetic sense: " 'Oh, so you're a lover of views, are you!' said
Skudronzhoglo,[49] suddenly looking at him severely. . . . Look for
utility and not beauty. Beauty will come of itself . . ." (p. 315).

These continuing references to matters of perception show
the self-consciousness of Part One raised to a more abstract
level: not a narrator calling attention to himself, but art calling
into question the bases of its own operation to serve the larger
moral allegory. Moral growth is compared with estate manage-
ment, and indeed Chichikov, once again leaving town in a
carriage, inspires the comparison of redemption to architecture:

> One might have compared the inner state of his soul
> with that of a structure that had been pulled down, but
> only for the purpose of putting up a new building from
> its materials; the new building had not been started yet,
> because a definite plan had not yet come through from
> the architect, and the builders are left without knowing
> what to do. (p. 365)

To pick up Gogol's metaphor, the architectonic pretensions of
Part Two are clear from the start: the text as Dantesque trilogy,
as cathedral, as icon of the evolving soul. But from start to
finish, one waits for the plans to arrive. The ambitious scheme
to use art to puncture the illusions of human artifice and thereby
reveal the artistry of the divine turns out to be a dead end,

perhaps because Gogol's new pieties were eroding the very irony required to make such a scheme succeed.

Selected Passages from Correspondence with Friends

Dead Souls, Part Two, cannot finally provide the answers to which it aspires, and *Selected Passages* (1847) largely concerns itself with that failure.[50] Among the letters' detailed prescriptions to Russians at large, over half the text concerns itself with literature, much of it Gogol's own writing. Here the spiritual and prophetic side of the author, seen before in *Annunziata*, comes clearly to view, and the terms are still recognizably Dantesque. In *Annunziata* the protagonist/narrator attains vision finally through the casting out of all voices but disembodied prophecy. In *Selected Passages* the even larger vision of Gogol's (and Russia's) own spiritual development echoes through an even more perfect soliloquy. With its preface, *Selected Passages* has thirty-three parts and begins and ends with the theme of pilgrimage toward which Part Two of *Dead Souls* moves. In his last letter, "Easter Sunday," Gogol unmistakably replicates Dante's own moment of emergence from the Inferno. As strongly as in the *Divine Comedy*, national destiny is seen to hinge on individual redemption; conversely, human art may be forgiven its imperfections until the Second Coming perfects the world that it depicts. As in the *Purgatorio* and in *Dead Souls*, Part Two, the artist becomes emblematic of the rhythms of salvation. Various artists (the starving engraver of "Testament," the painter Ivanov, Gogol himself, even the blind Homer) must suffer through to their reward. Gogol argues that delay itself can be formative, and we may be reminded of the souls learning patience on the ledges of the Mount of Purgatory. Redemption comes from loss:

> The second part of *Dead Souls* was burned because
> it was necessary. "Lest the seed die, it will not live

again," says the Apostle. It is first necessary to die in
order to be resurrected. . . . Immediately that the flame
had carried away the last pages of my book, its content
suddenly was resurrected in a purified and lucid form,
like the Phoenix from the pyre, and I suddenly saw in
what disorder was what I had considered ordered and
harmonious. (pp. 108–9)[51]

Though the burning of epics was a classical practice (Virgil,
Ovid), the sacrifice is here presented entirely in terms of Christian immolation and transfiguration.

One sees in *Selected Passages* explicit if not always convincing resolutions of problems that the second part of *Dead
Souls* has not yet brought under control. The pervasive uncertainties about the relationship of art and life underlie Gogol's
encomium of the painter Ivanov, who has (like Gogol in Rome)
been sacrificing his career and his life to complete a masterpiece
showing the movement of man to Christ, a canvas he cannot
complete until that movement finally happens. Gogol draws a
parallel at once to himself: "My works are strangely connected
to my soul and to my inner education. For more than six years
I could do no work for the world. All my work was done within
myself and for myself alone" (p. 152). The great strength of
Ivanov's work (and implicitly of Gogol's) lies in its directness
as spiritual expression; the question of a fit audience may be
postponed. Earlier, in talking about the public criticism of *Dead
Souls*, he similarly admitted that "my heroes are close to the
soul because they come from the soul; all my last works are the
story of my own soul" (p. 103). Indeed, the one passage of the
novel to which he explicitly refers is that moment of lyrical
reflection, discussed above, where Chichikov's consciousness and
that of the narrator seem to merge. Gogol now sits himself down
in Chichikov's carriage: "I have never been able to bear the doleful, lacerating sounds of our songs which rush across all of the
boundless Russian space. These sounds eat into my heart, and
I marvel that everyone is not aware of the same thing" (p. 99).

The autobiographical substratum of *Dead Souls* now comes clearly and undeniably to view, confirming Michael Holquist's claim that "the specific quality of Gogol's personal experience. . . which is at the center of his life and work, is a radical ontological rendering of self (*Zerrissenheit*)."[52] Gogol seems now to be experiencing in all seriousness the process, parodied at the end of *Dead Souls*, of losing track of the boundary between one's own fictions and the phenomenal world from which they derive. It is no longer literary form but salvation history that imposes limits on the utterance, for the text that can redeem society cannot appear, any more than can Ivanov's canvas, until there is a redeemed society to describe.

These rantings of the spiritual and prophetic Gogol reveal a writer who has thoroughly painted himself into a corner. Having admitted now to purely autobiographical fiction, as well as to ineffable spiritual purity, how is the writer ever to tell an interesting story? Yet he claims that he burned the sequel because it was too panegyrical: "To describe some fine characters who are supposed to demonstrate the nobility of our race would lead to nothing. It would only arouse empty pride and vanity" (p. 109).

Although a logical extension of the Dantesque turn of the end of *Dead Souls*, Part One, *Selected Passages* works as much to seal off that inner world of subjectivity and confession as to explore it. For the letters pursue the autobiographical mode to such an extreme that the voice talking about the voice talking about the voice becomes entirely disembodied. Having taken up the option offered by Christian confessional literature of presenting oneself as an Everyman, Gogol exaggerated it to the point where no particular personality at all shows through, no vivid scene of conversion, no delicious history of sins, no confession of continuing and individuating mortal weaknesses (apart from writer's block) such as Saint Augustine, Dante, and others made compelling. Given the confusions of text and world, the writer who creates the text asserts no more individuality than the Creator, whom he simultaneously expresses and assists. The letters, in fact, sound like nothing so much as the epistles of Saint Paul, also written from abroad, trying to promote faith and support temporal authority until the Second Coming, which in the closed universe of *Selected Passages* seems to be the advent of the sequel to *Dead Souls*.[53] Just as Gogol had to leave Russia in order to write about it, so he seems to confront the task of self-examination as virtually an exile from the self. Like Narcissus, he has vanished into his own reflection, having finally decided that it may be easier to issue a new Gogol than a new *Dead Souls*. The search for the third Rome gradually gives way to a search for a third Gogol, after what are now seen to be the false starts as storywriter and novelist.

Gogol has also found a way to keep his captious audience at bay by casting them in a kind of closet drama for which he writes all the lines. His fear of the audience had always surpassed that of most writers, often causing him to leave town when a new work appeared. The readers closing in on the narrator at the end of Part One of *Dead Souls*, even as the townspeople close in on Chichikov, are still a humorous fiction. But those earlier joking justifications of his scurrilous characters, such as we have cited above, are now repeated in dead earnest: "My heroes are not at all villains. . . . But the banality of all of them frightened my readers. . . . The Russian is more frightened of his insignificance than of all his vices and shortcomings. . . . None of my readers knew that while laughing at my heroes he was laughing at me" (pp. 103–4). Gogol has reversed the comedic stance taken at the end of Part One of *Dead Souls*—"Don't confuse me with my nasty characters!"—into a demand that readers make precisely that identification.

While *Dead Souls*, Part One, halts the action only occasionally (though increasingly) to address the audience, the whole of *Selected Passages* is an address to the readers—conceived of as individual recipients, or as social categories, or as Russia—to the exclusion of the fiction. The invented reader becomes the work's protagonist. However, Gogol's very stance of direct address unmediated by fiction and unclouded by pride shows careful rhetorical calculation: one would be caddish to criticize a writer who shows himself easily shattered by criticism. Self-criticism itself preempts outsiders' opinions. In taking what were in some cases letters that his perplexed, even angry, correspondents had received and presenting these messages as exemplary, working them into a pattern, arraying the now anonymous recipients into his own vision of a redeemed Russia— his own City of God—and by comparing, then finally confusing, their spiritual destiny with his own progress as a writer, Gogol manages to translate the audience from real (that is, the original recipients) to hypothetical.

The epistles of Saint Paul, when published, had a comparable effect in helping to translate a scattered collection of communions into an enduring ideal of Christendom. In recasting his troublesome audience into his own version of true (that is, Russian) Christendom, Gogol puts them on their best behavior. A communication from writer to reader so ritualized, so immersed in the matrix of religious language and obligatory charity, renders both parties ideal, innocuous, predictable. So inevitable is the Christian scenario, of course, that Gogol can supply everyone's lines—not only those for painters and writers, but even those for wives of provincial governors. In Part One of *Dead Souls*, Gogol had unexpectedly trapped the readers and the writer himself among the company of dead souls—a wicked but rather winning joke. *Selected Passages* implicates the reader in resurrection, a strategy equally fraught with contradictions without, however, the irony that held in suspension the contradictions of *Dead Souls*. The running joke of Captain Kopeikin's letters to the czar and Tentetnikov's grand and soon abandoned blueprint for the Russian nation now realizes itself in earnest. Gogol, while extolling humility, seems in fact to be replicating the animating act of the primal Ventriloquist who brought His creation to life by projecting His Word into it.

With the translation of self and audience into the controllable realm of the ideal comes the eradication of fiction. What Ivanov is painting is directly the Truth, mimetic to an extent that it cannot be completed until its subject matter (namely, redeemed humanity) completes itself. Gogol's feelings about his own involvement in belles lettres, in particular epic, can perhaps be read from "*The Odyssey* in Zhukovsky's Translation." The claims made for Homer's epic here fall little short of those for the Second Coming of *Dead Souls*, and in writing to Zhukovsky (December 14, 1849) Gogol observed, "At times it seems to me that the second volume of *Dead Souls* could serve for the Russian reader as a kind of step toward reading Homer."[54] Though pagan, the *Odyssey* comes to play a central role in salvation history, having been "Christianized, Gogolized and moralized into a conscious social blueprint," as Fanger observes.[55] The *Iliad*, the model for "Taras Bulba," now seems to Gogol just "an episode" (*Selected Passages*, p. 32). The *Odyssey*, by contrast, presents all of life. Like Christian revelation itself, it languished misunderstood in Europe, waiting for Russia to discover its ultimate riches. Now, in Zhukovsky's version, it is not just translated but reborn, reincarnated in "*the living word*" that even its first author did not hear, so that "all Russia might accept as its own . . . a miracle . . . a re-creation, a restoration, a resurrection of Homer" (p. 33).

Homer's purpose was not only to affirm "all the bewitching beauty of poetry" but also "to remind man that there is something better and holier in him." Gogol borrows from Dante and other Christian classicists not a few of the prophetic claims for pagan literature as parallel to and almost an extension of the Old Testament when he talks of how Homer could write "a living and complete book infused by law at a time when there was still neither law nor founders of order" (p. 36). But in seeing the *Odyssey* as the perfect and instructive model of patriarchal society, Gogol virtually manages to unmake it as a fiction. Although his own earlier tale of a traveling trickster descended from that very *Odyssey*, Gogol now looks squarely at the epic prototype and manages to unsee the fictive, playful, finally skeptical outlook that the reader finds in Homer's epic as much as in *Dead Souls*, Part One. Gogol's way of escaping from the dilemmas of his own fiction is to deny that fiction exists or, even back to the time of Homer, has ever existed. There is only scripture. Though celebrating the triumph of the life force, Gogol has, in the largely imaginary recipients of these unsent letters, found himself yet another set of dead souls.

Dead Souls, Part Two, implicitly diagnoses its own paralysis: Tentetnikov waits for another fit preceptor to appear; Chichikov waits for some blueprint for rebuilding his soul; Gogol waits for a plan to complete the immense cathedral of letters for which Part One can serve as cellar.[56] The solution here proposed is not to find another fit guide—the perfect critic that Pushkin should have lived to become—nor even to proceed without a guide, but for Gogol to become the critic himself and perhaps not proceed at all. In the pivotal eighteenth chapter, "Four Letters to Divers Persons Apropos *Dead Souls*," more or less at the midpoint of the book, Gogol scrutinizes both Part One and its critics, indeed even applies the allegories of the text to its misguided reception: "And if but one soul had begun to speak out in public! It was exactly as though everything had died out, as though Russia in fact was inhabited not by living but by *Dead Souls*" (pp. 97–98). His critics have taken his writing too literally, especially the "lyric digressions" of the intruding narrator, and have accused him of pride for the expansive assertions made. But he bears the responsibility for having issued an ill-made book prematurely, for relying on ironies that were misconstrued.

Pushkin plays an innocent role in this misadventure:

> It is enough for me to tell you that when I began to read the first chapters of *Dead Souls* to Pushkin, in the form in which they formerly were, Pushkin, who always

> laughed at my readings (he loved laughter), slowly
> became gloomier and gloomier, and finally he was
> completely somber. When the reading was finished, he
> uttered in an anguished voice: "God, how sad is our
> Russia!" This amazed me. Pushkin, who knew Russia
> so well, had not noticed that it was all a caricature and
> my own invention!...From this time forward I began to
> think only of how to mitigate the painful impression
> which *Dead Souls* had produced. (p. 105)

The surrounding discussion suggests that in heightening the
ironies and moving the characters closer to the banal, Gogol
threatened to irritate the Russian audience all the more. Alone
among mortals, Pushkin perceived Gogol's "principal essence,"
rivaled by no other writer: "the gift of representing the banality
of life so clearly, of knowing how to depict the banality of a
banal man with such force that all the *petty details* which escape
the eyes *gleam large* in the eyes" (p. 103). For all Pushkin's
insight, his death kept him from seeing everything: "Only after-
wards was it [Gogol's gift for the banal] deepened in me by its
union with some spiritual circumstance. But I was in no condition to reveal it then, even to Pushkin."[57] Gogol speaks here
as the perfect critic of his own work, of his critics, even of
Pushkin's wondrous critical insight. He has become the guide
that Pushkin did not live to be.

Even as his reading of the *Odyssey* implies that fiction does
not exist nor ever has, Gogol's retrospective profile of himself
as fiction writer presents that entity as little more than a result
of the audience's and his own confusions. When he thought he
was inventing fictions, he was actually stumbling upon the great
truth about Russia. It is his clumsiness, and his clumsiness
alone, that has upset people; but the Russian truth writes itself
without the imagination as an intermediary. In proof of this
thesis and in answer to the criticism of the troika scene at the
end of Part One, he simply rewrites that vision as fact:

> In Russia, now, it is possible to make oneself a
> hero at every step. Every rank and place demands
> heroism. . . . I perceive that great vocation which is not
> now possible for any other people, which is possible for
> the Russians alone, because before them alone is there
> such scope and their soul alone is acquainted with
> heroism—that is why that exclamation was wrenched out
> of me, and it was taken for vainglory and presumption!
> (p. 102)

To be sure, there is such a thing as literary craftsmanship, and
Gogol has nothing good to say about his own, even though
critics overlooked his careless stitching together of materials and
indecent rush into print. What they have criticized is beyond
criticism, for the Russian destiny announces itself, and his own
recognition of it was simply wrenched out of him, "an awkward
expression of a real feeling" (p. 99).

Literary criticism has produced few experiences odder than
hearing this unsurpassed ironist test and reject his work on the
touchstone of sincerity and monolithic truth. "My personal
thoughts, simple, unpuzzling thoughts, I did not know how to
transmit, and I myself gave grounds for these misinterpretations,
and on the harmful rather than the useful side" (p. 101). Part
One "is still no more than a prematurely born child" (p. 106).
Gogol does not see his work as an artifact, but rather as
something brought out from within, about which the author
can at most decide the moment of delivery. Though any creative
mind can feel itself transparent—as inspired, seized upon, spoken through—that passivity sounds strangest coming from an
ironist whose effects depend on obvious calculation. Though the
intruding narrator and the resultant voices within voices of Part
One raise introspection to the level of comedy, we dare not
assume that the eternal jokester who can mime and mock such
tones of desperate sincerity as we hear in the "lyrical digressions"
is not himself, at some level beneath and beyond the giddy play

of his levels and levels of irony, desperately sincere. What is most exhilarating about the authorial self of Part One as it radiates concentric and contradictory rings around itself—the narrator, Chichikov, Russia, Christendom, all clumsily allegorizing and bruising one another—is the deducible sense that here for once is a mind liberated, as ours cannot be, from the killing literalism of introspection. Here is a mind capable of leaping from ledge to ledge of its own abyss and looking back at itself without, like the rest of us, being sentenced always to experience consciousness on one flat, literal plain, without perspective and without proportion.

Selected Passages deflates that happy myth. Gogol discusses irony purely as a matter of communication, not introspection. His accounts of his relations with Pushkin and the Russian audience center on questions of irony. His observations about himself here, as in his earlier letters and in the half-fictionalization of those letters in "Rome," all proceed in the mode of unrelieved literalism. And indeed, the faltering of fiction in Part Two and the virtual exorcism of it in *Selected Passages* bring us back to the solemn, fragmented worlds of "Rome" and "Taras Bulba," the worlds, as we have seen, of Gogol narrating without irony. In its own labored and doctrinal terms, the self-abnegation of *Selected Passages* works toward the rapt passivity, the absorption into a perceived grandeur, of the ending of "Rome." The onerousness of the Russian identity in *Selected Passages* and its momentary absence in "Rome" commonly leave the artist with little to do with his illusion-making: in the latter case he lacks subjects; in *Selected Passages*, Russia's cooperatively manifest destiny has already done his work for him. In neither work is the reader constantly on the defensive, as in *Dead Souls*, lest pious affirmations suddenly be overthrown by abrupt shifts of perspective. The stringent hierarchies of *Selected Passages* recall the patriarchal and nationalist world of "Taras Bulba," again without fear of a shift to mockery. So ferocious is the authoritarianism of this Russia, both Cossack and Christian, that it threatens even to obliterate personality. In *Selected*

Passages the polarity between the pagan and confessional modes of monumental literature, "Taras Bulba" and "Rome," collapses under the weight of heroic and impersonal solemnity. If anything, the bardic anonymity of "Taras Bulba" shows more warmth and emotion than the inhuman dispassion (for all the pretense to confessional fervor) of the perfect critic who writes the letters, no longer Gogol but the daimon who has watched over his shoulder through misspent decades and now flies free to tell the tale or, as Gogol explains it, the "simple, unpuzzling thoughts" (p. 101) that have always lurked beneath his gifts for irony and illusion—gifts for which he now quite credibly claims to have found a cure.

Bakhtin's category of the "polyphonic" usefully illumines the evolution, or we might say attenuation, of the quality of voice in Gogol's writings in his last decade. The voices that begin *Dead Souls* are legion: earthy, pompous, rude, above all contentious, as they torture Russian prose into a particular brilliance. The emergent narrator asserts a more consistent literary discourse, and this discourse prevails, largely to the exclusion of dissonance and variety, in the long descriptive stretches of Part Two, fragments without drama because there are not enough voices to play it. *Selected Passages* marks the triumph of the monotone, the rejection of polyphony, as of irony and the world. As we have argued, this straitening into solemnity and consistency does not constitute a movement from the novelistic to the epic, but rather the sacrificing of the epic fiction's range and treachery, its evocation of many struggling voices so that one may impressively prevail. Gogol's faceless, official discourse might satisfy the theoreticians as epic but in fact mimes the voicelessness of scripture.

In a letter of December 29, 1847, Gogol described to Zhukovsky his literary impasse:

> For a long time I have been occupied by the thought of writing a *great work* in which I would present all that is

good and all that is bad in [the] Russian man and
thereby uncover before us the most obvious *quality* of
our Russian nature. Though I have seen and grasped
separately many of [its] parts, the plan of the whole has
just not unfolded itself to me or taken shape in the form
needed for me to begin writing it.[58]

In describing these uncooperative ideas and structures, he gives
no indication that he is waiting for a story to jell or characters
to evolve. We seem to be still among the ethical preachments
of *Selected Passages*. "At every turn I have felt that I am
lacking much, that I still can't tie and untie events, and that I
need to learn the structure of the great masters. I've taken them
up, starting with our beloved Homer." Bakhtin rightly observes
that Gogol undid himself in trying to write a dead literary form
but repeats Gogol's error in calling that form "epic."

Gogol's final drift to literal-minded prophecy, his renunciation of his narratives for some higher, more purely religious
and confessional form of artistic expression, anticipates an apparent syndrome that was to recur, if never again so acutely,
among masters of Russian monumental literature. Propelled by
the momentum of his own large creation, Tolstoy rejected *Anna
Karenina* (and no doubt *War and Peace* as well) when he insisted
to his friend V. V. Strakhov: "I assure you that this abomination
does not exist for me and that I am only vexed that there should
be people who have need of it."[59] "What Is Art?"—Tolstoy's
iconoclastic repudiation of the goals and methods of modern
fiction in the name of a simpler, more edifying, and universally
accessible aesthetic—could follow only after a statement such
as this, much as *Selected Passages* could issue forth only after
Gogol claimed in 1845: "I have no love for what I have written
and published up to now, and especially *Dead Souls*."[60] What
André Gide observed about Dostoevsky applies to other giants
of Russian prose: "The literary creator who seeks himself runs
a great risk—the risk of finding himself. From then onwards
he writes coldly, deliberately, in keeping with the self that he

has found. He imitates himself."[61] Gogol was only the first
Russian novelist to find himself in that frozen, infernal rut, but
also the first to show how monumental can be the journey that
leads to it. Even in failing to arrive at his heroic goal, he opened
the way for a tradition of Russian prose that adapts and extends
the classical and Christian modes of epic perhaps more successfully than any other modern literature. Of the innumerable
transmitters of Homer through the ages, Gogol seems among
the least likely, but it is in this role that Dostoevsky cast him
when he, too, took up the question of Whither Rus'? at the
end of his career. We turn now to *The Brothers Karamazov* as
another address to Gogol's great, unfinished project.

DOSTOEVSKY'S *THE BROTHERS KARAMAZOV* 3

For books continue each other, in spite of our habit of judging them separately.
——Virginia Woolf, *A Room of One's Own*

Like *Dead Souls*, *The Brothers Karamazov* was envisaged by its author as the first canticle of a Russian *Divine Comedy*. Both novels were conceived as multivolumed works about the life and spiritual rebirth of their sinner-heroes, Chichikov and Alyosha. Shortly before he began *The Brothers Karamazov*, Dostoevsky abandoned his idea for a master novel in five parts, entitled *The Life of a Great Sinner (Zhitie velikogo greshnika)*, which, recalling Gogol, he later termed a "real *poèma.*" "It will be my last novel, about the size of *War and Peace*," Dostoevsky wrote to A. N. Maykov. And further: "The main question which will run through all its parts is the very one I have struggled with consciously or unconsciously all my life—the existence of God."[1]

Although the project was conceived as early as 1869 and abandoned shortly thereafter, its fundamental theme remained with Dostoevsky until his death, partly surfacing in *The Devils* (1872) and even more so in *The Brothers Karamazov* (1880). "Fyodor Mikhailovich had great faith in this projected novel and considered it the culmination of his literary career," asserts Dostoevsky's widow in her reminiscences. "His pre-vision proved correct, since many of the characters of this novel figured later in *The Brothers Karamazov.*"[2] To Strakhov, Dostoevsky wrote about his grand scheme much as Gogol had written about *Dead Souls:* "I consider this novel to be the last work in my literary career."[3] And in his October 9 letter of the same year to Maykov, the writer admits, as Gogol had earlier confessed to Zhukovsky: "Being more a poet than an artist, I have chosen themes which are beyond my strength."[4] Of the applicability of Gogol's subtitle *poèma* not only to Dostoevsky's projected *The Life of a Great Sinner,* but to any of his late novels, Donald Fanger has recently noted: "One can hardly doubt the source of this term or the peculiar significance of the fact that Gogol's successor—not the author of *Poor Folk,* but of *Crime and Punishment, The Idiot, The Possessed, The Brothers Karamazov*—chose consistently to identify himself as a poet rather than a novelist."[5] Finally, both writers used the texts themselves to announce their projected sequels. Gogol announces in *Dead Souls,* Part One, that "there are still two long parts ahead of us" (p. 272), while Dostoevsky informs the reader in his preface to *The Brothers Karamazov* that it is the first part of a larger work, with Part Two, "the main novel," to follow shortly.[6] As we know, he did not live to complete the project.

As in Gogol, the sin, suffering, and redemption of the central character would bind together the different parts. In 1933, Pavel Bitsilli viewed Dostoevsky's sinner as an Everyman and, by placing *The Brothers Karamazov* in the tradition of Dante's epic, invited comparison to Gogol's fictively rendered inferno as well.[7] The German scholar N. Hofmann quotes Dostoevsky's widow regarding the plot for the unwritten sequel: "It was the author's plan for Alyosha...to take upon himself [the world's] suffering and its guilt.... After a stormy period of moral straying, doubt, and negation, Alyosha, left alone, returns to the monastery once more. There he surrounds himself with children and dedicates all the rest of his life to them, loves them truly, teaches and guides them."[8] As Fanger has argued but few

have explored: "If Gogol's significance for the young Dostoevsky
is a matter of record, the later record is no less indicative."[9]
Not only did his predecessor's Petersburg "nightmares," such
as "The Nose" and "The Overcoat," influence Dostoevsky's
earliest prose narratives, but it was Gogol's later, larger vision
of Rus' that would inspire and challenge him at the very end.

Quite in the Gogolian tradition, *The Brothers Karamazov*
is evasive about its literary legacy. Dostoevsky holds overt allusion to classical models to virtually only one strand: the
continuing preoccupation of Alyosha's boys with the founders
of Troy. In a novel where names are often significant to the
point of punning, the unremarkable scene where Kolya's class-
mate Dardanelov can only vaguely answer the question "Who
founded Troy?" may arrest the reader's attention, since Dardanelov, had he done his homework, should have identified
Dardanus (along with Tros and Ilus) as being among the various
generations of Trojan founders. On first reading one scarcely
knows whether or not to take this as one of the series of parables
of characters' failing to recognize their own identities, just as,
for example, Dmitri fails to account for the etymological link
of his name to Demeter in the myth of this goddess and her
daughter that he rehearses to Alyosha in "The Confession of
an Ardent Heart." Concerning the founders of Troy, even in-
genious Kolya is to be preempted by Kartashov, who figures
thereafter as "the boy who discovered about Troy most of all"
(p. 731).[10] This preoccupation with epic history seems a peripheral element of the childhood subplot until it becomes, in
the last chapter, the matrix within which the novel ends. As we
shall see, it may be a telling indication of where Dostoevsky
located himself in the epic cycle.

To investigate how *The Brothers Karamazov* presents itself
within the monumental tradition and as an extension of Gogol's
epic vision, we might first examine the reading habits that help
to discriminate one Karamazov from another. To some degree,
they are what they read as well as what they write. On the first

page of the novel, the narrator senses that Dmitri's mother went astray, like many another would-be Ophelia, as a result of reading European novels; bovarism thus emerges as the first threat to Russian identity. Her son, like Fyodor, shows himself much influenced by Schiller, whom he misreads. He sobs about the ode to Ceres (= the Greek Demeter) and Proserpina as if the focus (and an analogue for himself) were the poor, martyred daughter (just another Ophelia), and not in fact the grieving mother. As we shall see, his destiny is finally to see himself more in terms of his namesake, Demeter, and to recognize, as he fails to do in his effusion to Alyosha, that this is a myth not just of fall, but of resurrection. The Madonna and Sodom, between which Dmitri feels himself fatally trapped, have long since been reconciled in the redemption of Mary Magdalene, which Grushenka will embody to him. Like his mother, Dmitri begins by reading romantic literature, and reading it badly.

Ivan's devil has much to say about his reading habits, which are predictably broad and slanted toward rationalists and ironists, or so we gather when his demon finally divulges the sources of this not-so-original young intellectual: Voltaire, Heine, Pushkin, Tolstoy, and, above all, Ivan Karamazov. Of course, his demon derives less from the sins of these writers than from the way that Ivan has misappropriated them. His torment lies in being misquoted, twisted, and misused by his own muse, turned demonic, in precisely the ways that he himself has perfected. Whereas Dmitri and his mother misread to warrant misbehaving as they please, Ivan has used these texts as a justification for not acting at all. They reduce his interaction with people to "plotting," a mode of authorship that fails to engage Alyosha, who declines to play the role proposed to him by Ivan in "The Grand Inquisitor," but one that succeeds unwittingly and all too well with Smerdyakov.

With a demon like Ivan's, who has so much to say about his own literary origins, we miss Dante in the rogues' gallery beside Voltaire, Pushkin, and the others, although Gogol figures

briefly by allusion when the demon refers to himself as a "Khles-
takov" grown old (p. 608). Ivan had taken Dante as the literary
context for his poem about the Grand Inquisitor, but his absence
from the climactic delirium is telling, for he is the author best
at recognizing devils as such, while Ivan's torment consists in
his inability to define and excise his own demonic side. Of
authors cited by Dostoevsky, Gogol receives a second honor in
a demonic context: it was his *Evenings on a Farm Near Dikanka*
that Fyodor, in a wicked and witty gesture, gave to Smerdyakov
to stir his interest in books (p. 113).[11] Smerdyakov naturally
failed to see the humor. Though putting himself in the Dantesque tradition as he fictionalizes his own darker side in "The
Grand Inquisitor," Ivan similarly fails to see the humor, fails
to recognize that the devil is an ass, despite all the years Fyodor
has spent demonstrating that it is so. Ivan goes fatally wrong
in conferring tragic solemnity on such petty and pathetic figures
(the Inquisitor, Fyodor, and himself). Dmitri, who can laugh
as well as cry, finds a less pernicious fantasy in the absurdity
of seeing the Karamazovs as insects rather than tragic heroes.

The insect world of Dmitri, Ivan's denial of demons, and
the humor that Smerdyakov fails to grasp all point in the
direction of Gogol, whom Dostoevsky began his career by parodying in his short novels, starting with *Poor Folk* (1845) and
The Double (1846).[12] He begins and ends his masterpiece, *The
Brothers Karamazov*, with the various Gogolian questions posed
at the various Gogolian levels. The novel takes its epigraph
from John 12:24, "except a corn of wheat fall into the ground
and die, it abideth alone; but if it die, it bringeth forth much
fruit," the scriptural base of *Selected Passages from Correspondence with Friends*. Better than he knew, Gogol had thereby
aptly characterized the fertile death of his own narrative gifts—
fertile, that is, for his followers. By the end, *The Brothers
Karamazov* can rightly claim to take its birth from the deli-
quescence of Gogol's storytelling: the Public Prosecutor climaxes
his case against Dmitri, sarcastically, with Gogol's image of the

troika and the question, "Whither Rus'?". Yet the narrative
undercuts the Prosecutor's irony:[13] the troika—adumbrated in
Dead Souls as possibly the Holy Trinity, possibly Dante's Satan,
Brutus, and Cassius—has become flesh and dwelt among us in
the persons of Dmitri, Ivan, and Alyosha; and the question of
"Whither Rus'?" has been posed seriously by the trial. Though
answers had in the interval been found on the Tolstoyan scale
of war and peace, Dostoevsky pointedly returns to the Gogolian
scene of the crime. In both works we are confronted with a
nondescript provincial town, a rustic aristocracy, and a toy
version of a Russia that can turn in on itself in search of a
central enigma—Who was Chichikov? Who killed Fyodor?—
and instructively sort itself out for us by failing to grasp the
core of the answer: "ourselves."

That the reader should read *The Brothers Karamazov* in
the context of *Dead Souls* becomes clear also in the pivot of
the action, Dmitri's fatal rampage in Book 8, where his weird
journey recalls Chichikov's. For the moment, Dmitri becomes
a confidence man, trying to hock his patrimony, a scam scarcely
less dishonest or less macabre than Chichikov's acquisition of
dead souls. This midpoint and pivot of the plot, like Chichikov's
crucial visit to Pliushkin in *Dead Souls*, centers on the question
of time as embodied in a broken watch (hocked by Dmitri,
offered up as a gift by Pliushkin). Dmitri's visits to various
proprietary figures (Samsonov, Mme. Khoklakova, Lyagavy)
provide an array of dead souls to figure Russia in its various
modes of materialistic folly. At Mokroe, the question is squarely
posed whether the buffoon Maximov is the same as that in
Dead Souls. In both novels, the second half devotes itself to
conspiracy against and prosecution of the harmless rogues that
we know Chichikov and Dmitri to be. Both plots revolve, as
we have indicated, around riddles of identity: "Who is Chichikov?" (a veiled posing of the central question, "Who are these
dead souls?"); "Who killed Fyodor?" And the surrounding
groups, separated out by class, sex, and sophistication, reveal

the stratifications and respective delusions of Russian society as
they instructively fail to see their own responsibility. The similarity of these structures underscores the diametrical differences
of the topics at hand. In *The Brothers Karamazov* we have,
not a scam, but a real murder; not just a pretense to mortgage
the dead as if living, but a serious preoccupation with resurrection; not just a comic embodiment of Russianness, but a
publicized and influential test of Russian justice. Yet the mystical significances that Dostoevsky finds underlying Gogol's basic
structure are precisely those that Gogol himself looked back to
and found after 1842.

To be sure, the ramification of allegory in *The Brothers
Karamazov* has little enough to do with Gogol even in his later
mystagogic phase. With an elaboration worthy of Dante himself,
the troika, the holy and unholy trinity, becomes not just the
three brothers and their respective women, but eventually three
confessions, three temptations, three lacerations, three torments,
three visits to Smerdyakov. Yet in explaining his system of
symbols, the relating of large and small that allows the individual
to figure Russia and thereby figure Christendom, Dostoevsky
allies himself with Gogol in opposition to Tolstoy. That trenchant
but tendentious literary critic, Ivan's devil, presents himself as
Tolstoy's muse—that is, whatever combination of delirium and
dyspepsia allows a brilliant mind to grasp both the large and
small without grasping their organic link:

> Listen, in dreams and especially in nightmares, from
> indigestion or anything, a man sometimes sees such
> artistic visions, such complex and real actuality, such
> events, even a whole world of events, woven into such a
> plot, with such unexpected details from the most exalted
> matters to the last button on a cuff, as I swear Leo
> Tolstoy could not create.... (p. 606)

The demonic characters in the novel uniformly mark themselves
out as literalists who fail to grasp the metaphoric and devel-

opmental connections that can exist between large and small, microcosm and macrocosm. Smerdyakov, in the midst of his dinner-table casuistries, centrally distorts the terms in which the mustard seed and the mountain are meant. Ivan, rescued by Alyosha from his devil, indicates how a better grounded but not less pernicious physicalism has enthroned itself in science, in his delirious jumbling of seraphim and molecules: "Dmitri calls you a cherub! Cherub!...the thunderous howl of the seraphim. What are the seraphim? Perhaps a whole constellation. But perhaps that constellation is only a chemical molecule" (p. 618).

Ivan's devil also recalls the dialectic of destruction and rebirth announced in the novel's epigraph from John 12:24. Even in parodying the Christian sense of miracle, the devil articulates an alternative to the dissociating visions of science and intellectualism: "I shall sow in you [Ivan] only a tiny grain of faith and it will grow into an oak tree..." (p. 612). The small and the large can be related, then, not just by scientists with microscopes and telescopes or by authors like Tolstoy with notebooks to catalogue and organize buttons and battalions, but by the germinal powers of the childlike, the latent, the absurd, and the believed. As a symbol of redemption, Grushenka's onion also provides an image for symbolic structure, the rings-within-rings of signification within the narrative, as within the mind and the nation. Whether it is faith or irony that grows one layer from another resists explanation; the oak and the acorn stand in as absurd a relationship as that of the mountain and the mustard seed. Yet Dostoevsky more than hints that, if it were left to Tolstoyan objectivity, molecules could never grow into constellations nor families into nations. For nations and constellations are more than accumulations, as Zosima can perceive even in the ocean: "...for all is like an ocean, all is flowing and blending; a touch in one place sets up a movement at the other end of the earth" (p. 299). As the epigraph reminds us, without dirty work there is no growth for seeds, nor for unsoiled lives or literal understandings. In stark contrast to Tolstoy's immaculate version of history, what came out from under Gogol's overcoat to riot through Skotoprigonevsk was legion.

Before considering the implications of Dostoevsky's use of *Dead Souls* for the structure of *The Brothers Karamazov*, let us recall Gogol's bestiary, and in particular the possibility that the insect world—the teeming, squirming mites that draw Dostoevsky's eye as they do Gogol's[14]—has its own direct link to the monumental tradition. As we saw with the opening simile of *Dead Souls*, the comparison of the socialites at the governor's ball to flies promenading over a sugar loaf, it is the most irreverent narrative jabs that turn out to convey heroic force most directly. With Gogol's flies and Dostoevsky's Karamazov insects we would seem to be at a polar remove from the high style that Homer initiated. Rather than seeing provincial dignity (Gogol) or degradation (Dostoevsky) in terms of creepy crawlies, Homer famously confers dignity and lyricism even on carnage. In *Iliad* 16, Sarpedon, the son of Zeus, falls mightily and, as the potter Euphronius recalls, Sleep and Death fly him from the fray at the bidding of his bereaved father. "Good night, sweet prince, and flights of angels sing thee to thy rest." Yet in the Homeric imagination, Sleep and Death were not the only winged creatures in this grand, sad moment:

> No longer
> could a man, even a knowing one, have made out the
>   godlike
> Sarpedon, since he was piled from head to ends of feet
>   under
> a mass of weapons, the blood and the dust, while others
>   about him
> kept forever swarming over his dead body, as flies
> through a sheepfold thunder about the pails overspilling
> milk, in the season of spring when the milk splashes in
>   the buckets.
> So they swarmed over the dead man....
>
> (*Iliad* 16.637–44)[15]

Homer's and Gogol's swarming flies are not entirely different. On the windy, odorless plain of Troy, where bodies tear and burst but do not putrefy, and fall prey to the clean excarnation of dogs, birds, and fishes (and that only in baleful warnings, never in depicted scenes), the image of flies swarming over a corpse is daringly potent as the reality most familiar to the audience and best suppressed by this poem. What darkens and enriches the fantasy of Sarpedon preserved incorruptible, as if turned into a statue, and carried off by Sleep and Death is the simile of flies on a corpse. Death is death, and even for the sons of gods admits of only insignificant variations. Some of the most powerful effects of the high style, even in the definitive Homer, issue from low subjects.

To persist a moment with the millennial history of the Entomological Sublime, which in monumental literature may be argued to culminate in Dostoevsky, the simile of the swarming flies in *Iliad* 16 serves centrally to widen perspective from the duel of Sarpedon and Patroclus to the much larger canvas of the battle over the corpse. A wasp simile had been used earlier to describe the numbers and fury of Achilles' men when they are finally allowed to resume fighting:

> The Myrmidons came streaming out like wasps at the
>   wayside
> when little boys have got into the habit of making them
>   angry
> by always teasing them as they live in their house by the
>   roadside;
> silly boys, they do something that hurts many people;
> and if some man who travels on the road happens to
>   pass them
> and stirs them unintentionally, they in heart of fury
> come swarming out each one from his place to fight for
>   their children.
> In heart and in fury like these the Myrmidons streaming
> came out from their ships. . . .
>
>   (*Iliad* 16.259–67)

Implicit in Homer's image of the very small, the wasps, is the notion of the very large. The audience's memory of having seen and felt the pure horror of such tiny, ferocious swarms makes the army of Myrmidons seem incomprehensibly larger.

Parallels abound. The biggest single percussion in the epic is that of Apollo knocking over the Greek wall as easily as a boy kicks down a sand castle (*Iliad* 15.362–64). What better referents have we for imagining the scale and freedom of gods on earth, their wantonly enormous advantages over human striving, than children and their toys? The breaching of the wall marks a climax, made all the grander by the contrast to the inconsequent world of youth. More's the horror that this is anything but child's play, that walls serve finally for the casting down of Hector's son and other conquered children. But the poet leaves all such reactions to contrast. Enormity must be deduced from child's play, as oppositely elsewhere from hugeness—similes of oceans, forest fires, tumbling boulders. Such are the familiar eccentricities of an epic whose unrivaled Achilles sometimes compares himself to a wolf or lion, sometimes to a mother bird. The *Iliad* looms so large in memory, not because it makes any steady use of bigness or smallness, but because we never know quite what to expect. In all seriousness the *Iliad* can present Athene in Book 17 (570ff.) as possessing "the persistent daring of that mosquito / who though it is driven away from a man's skin, even / so, for the taste of human blood, persists in biting him."

Of course, ounce for ounce, mosquitoes suffer no comparison in ferocity to lions and wolves. And if one asks what is the epic animal par excellence, though the Hellenist would automatically propose Homer's silent lions, it is the insects which inherit the epic earth, because they above all pose the questions of scale and energy that have to preoccupy the heroic poet. We recall, in *War and Peace*, Tolstoy's comparison of Moscow to a queenless and doomed hive, a simile that derives ultimately from Virgil's comparison of the Carthaginians to bees when

Aeneas first arrives and from Dido's perception of the departing Trojans as ants. Between Virgil and Tolstoy, Milton, in the first book of *Paradise Lost*, shrinks Satan from the shiplike Leviathan on the fiery lake to the insect-sized being who can fit with myriads of peers into Pandemonium. Here is the locus classicus of demonism as literalism, for the swarming devils are not just compared to bees but in the process actually become bee-sized. From medieval notions of Beelzebub to Dmitri's Karamazov-vermin, somehow insects manage to say more about what is perverse in man or his world than do lions and boars: quoth Gloucester, "As flies to wanton boys are we to th' gods / They kill us for their sport" (*King Lear* IV.i. 36–37).

Dostoevsky, like Gogol, forces us to distinguish monumentality from grandeur and to recall that the big impact of epic relies not on the bigness of what is described but on the paradoxes of finding the immense in the minuscule, the sublime in insects, evil in insignificance. What is not to be relied on, apart from the aggrandizing distortions of retrospect, is any quantifiable weight of words, or the cast of thousands, or days and days of hacking. Epic focuses much more on the active contrasting of big and small, of grand and inconsequential, which tends not to be an axis of central importance to novelistic fiction. As a low-grade romantic and a sloppy reader of Schiller, Dmitri fits comfortably in the world of the novel. But his imaginative range, not just along the axes of good and bad (the Madonna and Sodom) but of the grand and the slight (Mother Earth and the insect), reaches also into the monumental tradition.

We have seen Gogol's concluding fumble to be the most telling narrative gesture, the inability at the end of a volume either to stop the tale conclusively or to continue on to volume 2 in a way consistent with the assumptions of what precedes. The concluding question of *Dead Souls*, Part One, much as it would seem to open the way to a sequel, provides unexpectedly inviolable closure, to be reopened, if at all, through criticism, theory, or apology, but not storytelling. When we come to *The Brothers Karamozov* as yet another first canticle of some Russian *Divine Comedy*, we may well ask the following: along with the Gogolian questions and the Gogolian subject matter, did Dostoevsky not also inherit from *Dead Souls* the tendency for a certain open-ended view of experience to seal itself off narratively beyond hope of continuation? Does the novel not end with beginnings, as did Dante in the circular structure that leads from the end of the *Paradiso* to the beginning of the *Inferno*? Dostoevsky's concluding questions may in fact provide closure as final as Gogol's.

To end with the childhood theme, as Dostoevsky does, suggests such circularity. As we have argued with reference to Tolstoy and Pasternak, the orderly and classicizing monumentalists in the Russian tradition inherit classical epic's usual inability to find a single ending faithful both to the public and to the private concerns between which it presumes to discriminate.[16] Reunion with Penelope is one sort of ending; pacifying Ithaca, quite another. With the same awkwardness, *War and Peace* ends once with Natasha and Pierre, then again and again with historical epilogues. Ivan's devil reminds us that Tolstoy can so magisterially get buttons and battalions onto the same canvas only through rigid assumptions about the bigness of the big and smallness of the small, the constellation and the molecule. Much as Tolstoy would like to reassign values between big and small, Napoleon and his head cold, of Russian stylists he is the least inclined to tamper with proportions. The more phantasmagorical and oneiric imaginations of Gogol and Dostoevsky jumble scale, let the public be swallowed up by the private, the private by the mind, and the mind by the universal (for Russia is spirit)—the universal itself being subsumed back into the public in this coiled reality always swallowing its own tail. By virtue of the dense network of sympathies, emanations, and ghosts that bind together their little nowhere/everywhere worlds, Gogol and Dostoevsky are therefore the more capable— and more capable than they may quite have liked—of finding a closing chord in which all that precedes can resonate. We shall end with Dostoevsky's ending.

Before proceeding with the comparison of Dostoevsky to Gogol, however, we must also recognize that one of Dostoevsky's most un-Gogolian aspects is the extent to which he has completed the Gogolian project. He has gone further than his predecessor in reconciling the satiric and the redemptive and in finally working fiction into salvation history in a way that mends the rupture between *Dead Souls*, Part One, and *Selected Passages*. We do not, as with Gogol, have a brilliant, crazy tale followed by years of exegesis, but rather the unfolding of both modes together. Mostly from the mouths of the brothers themselves, we have our lectures as we go along. It is a received truth of literary history that Gogol's breakthrough to psychological analysis is brought to an unrivaled consummation by Dostoevsky. Not just Maximov, but all the other dead souls have found a new home in Skotoprigonevsk.[17]

Looking at Dostoevsky's use of Gogol in more detail, we shall find that he has in some ways reversed the arc of Gogol's career, moving from autobiography back to myth,[18] from linear to cyclical time. Where Gogol announced emergent nationhood in the concluding "Whither Rus'?" Dostoevsky submerges that chauvinism back into a larger meditation on nationhood that leads back simultaneously to the Sermon on the Mount and the founding of Troy—that is, in the latter case, to the beginning of the epic cycle here being concluded yet again. We shall need to follow in some detail that shift in narrative time.

In *Dead Souls*, Part One, as we have seen, a narrative that starts in the cyclic time of myth moves toward the stronger lines of causation of autobiography. The various landowners could be reshuffled in the narrative, decimated, or augmented without disrupting the flow; the plots can be encountered in any order in this provincial cemetery. With Pliushkin, time enters the narrative, Chichikov gains a biography, and the narrator emerges into self-consciousness and moves toward

autobiography. The first six books of *The Brothers Karamazov*
mark a clear movement along this Gogolian axis, beginning
with the capsule biographies of the brothers. These factual and
detached sketches largely leave the Karamazovs' motives, as
well as their interrelationships, to be established, as happens
in the early scenes. The centripetal, psychologizing, inward-
looking values of the final movement of *Dead Souls* form, then,
the first narrative movement, though the emergent narrator is
conspicuously absent. The psychological filling-out does not
affect all characters equally. As we see in the monastery scene,
the traitors (here Rakitin, as later Ivan) reveal themselves fully,
while the redeemers (Zosima, and in his wake Alyosha) reveal
only more and more of their enigmatic natures. The climax of
this opening movement, as Dostoevsky himself indicated[19] is
reached in Book 5, with Ivan's poem about the Grand Inquisitor
and its answer in the Life of Zosima. The outlook and style of
the opening narrative culminate in Ivan, whose psychologizing
supplants faith. As a creator of fictions and poser of unan-
swerable questions—why must children suffer?—he embodies
the powers of Dostoevsky himself as narrator.

The questions posed by Ivan in the one style are answered
in quite another by Alyosha, whose literary style in itself does
not concede Ivan's basic assumptions. The saint's life, wherein
the meaning of Zosima's experience is distilled by Alyosha, does
not proceed in the historical time of the narrative, where every
moment is to be accounted for (even, as in Part Four of this
novel, accounted for repeatedly in explaining Fyodor's murder),
and where the causal link of one event to another is decisive.
Hagiography presents instead moments when the divine inter-
sects with the human; and these moments, far from being links
in a chain, need not be recounted in chronological order or as
a causal succession among themselves. For each such moment
testifies independently to a higher truth, so that even a partial
catalogue of them, like Alyosha's unfinished Life of Zosima, is
fully meaningful. Nor is there any need for a full account of

human psychology, as is apparent in Alyosha's telling of the high points of Zosima's experience: Markel's death, Zosima's duel, his mysterious stranger. As a text encapsulating the character of its author, Alyosha's Life of Zosima follows in the wake of Dmitri's ardent confessions, Smerdyakov's casuistries, and Ivan's "poem" of the Grand Inquisitor as Alyosha's central self-identification. Each of the brothers is an author in his characteristic way: Dmitri with drunken spontaneity, Smerdyakov with lethal calculation, Ivan with calculated vulnerability. For his part, Alyosha, like the Christ who does not speak to the Grand Inquisitor and like the gospel writers who assume no persona in their own narratives, eludes attention as much as his brothers seek it. His anonymous detachment, his redemptive passivity in relation to the narration, marks a polar opposite to Ivan's thinly disguised self-fictionalization in the Grand Inquisitor and his inability to provide allegories of anything but himself, leading to the final claustrophobia of his inability to produce a devil that is other than a mirror. Well before Ivan meets this other self, Alyosha has articulated and controlled his own alter ego in the hagiography of Zosima.

In the movement from psychological biography to saint's life, Dostoevsky reverses the movement of *Dead Souls*, Part One, from the flattened, atemporal perspective of its first half to a self-revealing narrator who, like Ivan, projects his own torments onto the tale. Gogol, as we have seen, had to depart fiction altogether to continue with the project of self-examination and self-justification. *Selected Passages* went on to break down and answer, area by area, the question of "Whither Rus'?" in the mode of confession. Moving from Ivan to Alyosha, Dostoevsky can address the large national issues still within the form of his novel. He recasts Gogol's homiletics as saint's life to capture Russia's future through the lens of its literary origins.[20] In the contrast of narrative styles between Ivan and the self-effacing Alyosha lies a justification for the problematic elusiveness of the narrator of the novel's events of thirteen years before.

Characteristic of both *Dead Souls*, Part One, and *The Brothers Karamazov* is that the narrative splits at the center, though in rather opposite ways. As we have seen, the central point of *Dead Souls* leads to the intrusion of a narrator, as the succession of landowners comes to an end with Pliushkin. In the reminiscently Gogolian Book 8, Dmitri's capture and delirious dream initiates what might be called an angelic counterplot, for which "The Russian Monk" has provided a sort of scriptural basis. This other, increasingly independent plot concerns children. Dmitri in his dream of the babe spiritually gives his proxy to Alyosha. Fixed and immobile as he is, Dmitri forfeits the ability to mediate in action between the faith of Alyosha and the rationality of Ivan. The narrative movements that were drawing Alyosha closer into the plot (chiefly at the end of Book 4, with the series of lacerations around him) fail to develop, and his ministry to the children proceeds as a largely unconnected narrative foil—or, at least, unconnected in comparison to the increasingly densely woven narrative strands within the crime and punishment plot.

Two strands in the narrative proceed for the most part separately. On the one hand, we have the implicit continuation of the Life of Zosima, now centered on Alyosha; and, on the other, we have the enactment of Ivan's scenario for the Grand Inquisitor—not just in the temptations of Smerdyakov to which Ivan immediately and unwittingly falls prey, but in the whole courtroom full of inquisitors who ask the wrong questions. The latter crime and punishment plot develops like a noose tightening around Dmitri: the facts are ferreted out until the truth becomes irrecoverable. Ivan's understandings close in until they collapse onto themselves. For those who insist on rational causality, and the law does so insist, the explanations become so dense as to be indecipherable or unbearable. But such, in the Christian view, has always been the limit of the law in contrast to the

workings of grace, and the childhood theme speaks powerfully,
though it is constantly interrupted and lacks central narrative
links. The loose ends are not a structural flaw but a tribute to
the paratactic style of saint's life, early epic, and myth, forms
of discourse in which events placed one after (but not because
of) the other gain eloquence from the power of shared cultural
values, the common agreement about the benign gods, or the
tragic mortal limits that shape all experience.

The responsibility, the legal or novelistic "Who did it?"
for Ilyusha's death is never worked out as it is for Fyodor's,
since causation must yield to meaning, and meaning is clear.
Like Alyosha in writing Zosima's life, the narrator is anonymous
within this strand, while he is increasingly self-revealing in his
report of the trial: we know he was there; he tells us directly
what he sees and does not see and what he knows now with
the advantage of thirteen years of hindsight. Were he to provide
such hindsight for Alyosha's boys, that information would have
incomparably greater impact, for those years of maturation
would dispel the ambiguities of their young natures. Alyosha
organizes his homily on memory around the theme of "whatever
happens to us in later life," that is, on the uncertain prospects
of whether they will turn out well or ill and perhaps not even
meet again for twenty years. That uncertain prospect is left as
pointedly unresolved as Gogol's concluding "Whither Rus'?"
Otherwise the youths' mysterious potential would evaporate,
and the final implications of Kolya's precocity would explain
themselves. This strand of narrative, the childhood plot in the
wake of hagiography, does not concern itself with results of that
sort. Such information is all that matters to Ivan and the various
other inquisitors in the crime and punishment plot, for lives
cannot be measured otherwise. Boys matter only by virtue of
the men they become. From the nonhierarchical standpoint of
Zosima, such eventualities matter little: the boys are not less
themselves as youths than they will be as adults; the boy Kolya

has an identity beyond the consuming question of whether he will turn into a saint or a monster.

The two plots, then, articulate different views of the world in contrasted styles and proceed with different rhythms. The trial brings the rationalizing and psychologizing narrative to implosion. Knowledge is destroyed, the characters succumb one by one to paralysis, and Russia becomes less herself. In its plotlessness, the childhood plot is, to an equal and opposite degree, expansive and liberating. Whereas the centripetal pressures of the trial and of Ivan's introverted rationality reveal the dark, anarchic centers of Dmitri, Ivan, and contemporary Russia, Alyosha suffers no such explanation because, in his current angelic mode, his center is everywhere. By the final chapter we have come back to the subject of the first chapter: the lives of boys—once the three Karamazovs, now these other twelve. The empty frame that we have seen filled, unacceptably, by psychologizing and rational analysis, is now seen as filled again by collective spirit and suprarational participation in timeless realities, the replication through Alyosha and the twelve boys of both the Sermon on the Mount and, as we shall see, the rituals of heroic memory.

To look now at the conclusion, *The Brothers Karamazov* ends on a double note, as is typical of monumental structures. Looking to the epic tradition, we might first be inclined to diagnose the opposition as being between public and private: the inquisitors and the children, the world of Ivan and the world of Alyosha. Yet the distinction is not between public and private, and therefore finally beyond resolving, but between adults and children, fathers and sons. The reuniting of fathers and sons that resolves Homer's plots and resonates throughout the subsequent tradition may figure equally in the distinctive concerns of the modern novel. Indeed, Michael Holquist sees filiation as the theme through which *The Brothers Karamazov* resolves the dilemmas of Dostoevsky's earlier novels:

in his last novel he was to go beyond the unbridgeable
antitheses of such models [*imitatio* of *Geist* or *imitatio
Christi*], to find a way out of the narrative dilemma
defined by the absolute hegemony of self (*The Idiot*), the
absolute hegemony of the others (*The Possessed*), or the
absolute hegemony of the Completely Other *(Crime and
Punishment)*. A man cannot become a God, absolute ego
cannot become another, but a son may become a father,
which is the progression of *The Brothers Karamazov*.[21]

The adult world has incriminated itself, has choked on its own
overabundant answers, on too many plots. The inheritors, however, need no narrative development. Alyosha never finished his
Life of Zosima, but we can scarcely tell where it leaves off, nor
do we much regret the loss. That life is not in need of added
chapters because its pattern is clear. To the degree that it is
scriptural, it bids not to be ended but to be lived. That "life"
is the incorporeal and unstinking remains of Zosima, reincarnated in Alyosha and in any others who enact its truths. It is
finally independent of narrative time because, as the source of
life—the Logos that was in the beginning—rather than its memorial, it is not ultimately narrative. It does not need further
plot any more than the acorn needs an instruction booklet. With
the relationship of large and small, the relationship of the one
and the many may be taken as understood: having come to
understand the acorn and the oak, we have little need to wait
around to watch a bushel turn into a forest.

Because of its brief and intermittent nature, we may be
tempted to label the childhood theme as the counterplot. Yet
that purely diagnostic literary judgment embodies precisely the
kind of literalism that Dostoevsky is teaching us to avoid. The
childhood theme is not a foil for the murder story, but rather
the matrix within which it exists. For in this case the children,
Alyosha and the twelve, are the fathers of the men, and the
realities encountered among them are prior and causal. They
provide explanation when the judicial inquiry voids itself. Each

plot centers on a death that may be read as sacrifice, but they inspire different questions: *Who* killed Fyodor? *Why* did Ilyusha die? As we see in the long and erroneous working out of the official investigation, the question of "who?" encourages deductive thinking that succeeds only in concealing its own fallaciousness. Seekers of causation are baffled by the fact that too many causes can be found. Finger pointers go wrong in failing to realize that quite a number of people are responsible for Fyodor's murder, including themselves. For Ilyusha's death, however, a worthy interpreter is to be found in Alyosha, who does not deductively sort out causes but celebrates the meaning of what has happened in a formalized ritual of memory that reenacts the origins of literature, as of religion. Memory, seen serving Ivan demonically for delusion and escape, can also be the act of taking responsibility. This final scene of foundation, far more than resolving just this particular tale, leaps to an explanation of why such tales are told or ever have been told.

Along with the two plots and the two narrative styles, two explanations of the origins of culture compete in the tale. As Michael Holquist has observed, the killing of Fyodor partakes of that primal killing of the father that, in other terms, Freud in *Totem and Taboo* took to be the origins of culture, a sacrifice lately analyzed in religious terms by René Girard.[22] Yet the cultural yield of this death is purely negative: it reveals the brothers' respective failures to take responsibility and lures rationalists into a search for causes that are doomed to endless confusion among the intertwined, redundant, and indecipherable strands of responsibility. Yet Fyodor's death poses strangely few questions about the mysteries of human life: everyone is better off with him dead. The very respect for fatherhood, as for brotherhood, that has to be affirmed by the brothers' process of taking responsibility condemns Fyodor more tellingly than his resentful sons ever managed to do. In and of itself, his death manifests a just and cooperative universe; the vipers consume each other. For the death of Ilyusha, by contrast, one cannot even begin to sort out the causes, for the loss can never be explained or justified either rationally or emotionally. This loss does not allow the universe to be sorted out into familiar and reassuring hierarchies. Among other things, in this case the child can see and bear the meanings far more than can his deformed parents. Ilyusha's death belongs to a different category of sacrifice, that of sons rather than fathers, which rivals the actions of Freud's primal horde as an explanation of culture.[23]

Two cultural traditions center on this sacrifice, the biblical and the classical heroic, and Dostoevsky invokes both to round out the novel—or, rather, to leave the ending monumentally open and generative. To trace out his use of biblical paradigm we must return to "The Russian Monk" and its relationship to the subsequent narrative. Holquist has aptly compared Alyosha's biography to a frame without a picture, a field waiting to be filled. Among its omissions is Zosima's particularly fragmentary representation of Job, a Job whose endurance, along with God's rewards for that endurance, is omitted. The plot provides two enactments of Job's role to explain the omission. The one is the disconsolate Snegiryov, as distraught and destroyed by the death of children as is Ivan. Ivan, in "The Grand Inquisitor," invokes insoluble questions like Job's about why he must suffer. Job turns out to be at the bottom of the eternal grudge borne by Ivan's devil: "How many souls have had to be ruined and how many honorable reputations destroyed for the sake of that one righteous man, Job, over whom they made such a fool of me in old days" (p. 615). The other enactment of Job's role is Alyosha, who has assumed the surrogate paternity of the boys that Zosima assumed for him. His ability to confer meaning on the death of Ilyusha in the absence of an explanation recalls the New Testament answer to Job through a Creator who has lost his own son. Here the most characteristic and least welcome aspects of the mortal condition—anguish, loss, and the chilliest insights into the void of explanations—assimilate suffering mortals to the very experience of the divine. The god in this case has set the pattern for human suffering at the cost of his own son, that is, not so much by imposing sacrifice, as long ago in the testing of Abraham and Job, as by experiencing it himself and bequeathing it. The dignity of gods and men is commonly achieved.

Within the theology of the novel, taking responsibility for the death of the father is not the final step. Ivan and Dmitri have both done so but remain confused and desolate. Such responsibility does lead to a rebirth of fraternity, yet the perception that we are our brothers' keepers remains still within the enlightened legalism of Genesis—that is, still literalistic, partial, and unredeemed. Alyosha has proceeded to the new dispensation by taking responsibility for the death of the son, the step whereby sons become fathers and the step whereby the New Testament sets itself apart from the Old. The essence of madness and torment for Ivan is to be confronted with offspring (for instance, his ideas, Smerdyakov) that he will neither acknowledge nor take responsibility for. Like Lucifer (also incensed by the ambiguities of his Creator), they rise up against their maker. Ivan remains fixed and tormented in a stance that is reactive and filial. The beginnings of salvation for Dmitri lie in perceiving in different terms the myth of his namesake, Demeter (Ceres), and Proserpina that he once presented to Alyosha as the key to his identity in "The Confession of an Ardent Heart." In his self-absorption and longing for annihilation, Dmitri identified himself then with the lost daughter, Proserpina. In the dream of the child, he now progresses to the sorrowful vision of the mother.

In showing Alyosha with the boys, the last chapter of the novel, then, is not just a sentimental set piece, but an unprecedented act in what turns out to be the privileged (because explanatory) plot in the novel. Alyosha takes responsibility for Ilyusha's death by shouldering the burden of explaining its meaning (but, emphatically, not its causes) and enacts that meaning in ceremonial remembrance. What derives from Il-

yusha's death, as not from Fyodor's, is worship rather than
deductive explanation and a ritual of memory predicated on
praise and blame rather than on analysis. It is not just the
possibilities of Christ among the apostles that Alyosha renews
among his own twelve, for the scene has Homeric antecedents
as well. The ritual spontaneously regenerated here lies behind
the earliest traditions of heroic verse. Herein the recurring
references to the founders of Troy and the name of Dardanelov
(recalling the Trojan founder, Dardanus) explain themselves. In
these scenes among the consolidating youths are inherent not
only the origins of Russia, but also the origins of Europe in
Troy. And Alyosha's cult of memory is also the origin of heroic
poetry, the *klea andrōn*, the "glories of men," that lie behind
the monumental tradition, here flowering yet again.

If psychological explanation is one of the characterizing
modes of the novel, then in taking psychology beyond itself in
The Brothers Karamazov Dostoevsky has also taken the novel
beyond itself, back to the prototype of heroic poetry from which
it ultimately derives. In significant ways, the boys exist outside
of the bourgeois society that is the source and subject of the
novel as a modern form. As an all-male and not yet sexually
active group, they exist before and outside of questions of sexual
difference, domestic obligations, and rivalry over women. Their
gregariousness is only now being challenged by disputes over
property and class (the dog Perezvon, Ilyusha's poverty), but
may still withstand the threat. Though youth can narratively
serve the definition of middle-class manners and values by
depicting the process of their absorption, such is not the direction
in which these boys are being led by Alyosha as chief educator
and authority figure. As a gang they still have the capacity for
collective feeling and action that comes to be perceived as a
fatal absence in adult society.

The boys, then, form a group apart from the typical concerns of the novel, even beyond its central explanatory use of
individual psychology. Attacking Ilyusha, they embody the pri-

mal horde that the Karamazov brothers symbolize only at an allegorical remove. Along with their comparative freedom from the preoccupations of property, class, and manners, the boys exist in a mode of time that novels normally cannot accommodate. With the benign inexperience of youth, they think themselves immortal; as a horde, they *are* immortal, for the gang will eternally replicate itself with new faces and eternally fail to learn the error of its ways. Dostoevsky has isolated that part of any society, Russian or other, in which the primordial questions of myth can be confronted without the distractions of politics, decorum, or philosophical self-seeking. For the boys, the death of Ilyusha is Death itself coming into the world, as Markel's was for Zosima; for them, Alyosha's preaching is the definitive experience of the Messiah, as his own memory of his mother before the icon contains the very experience of the Madonna. The narrative issues are confronted with the distillation and immediacy of heroic poetry. Such is the single-sex, fraternally bonded, primally vicious, and primally charitable cohort of boys, as of fraternal warriors.

This final scene of unrelated individuals constituting themselves as a family by virtue of accepting responsibility as fathers and sons echoes precisely the last note of the *Iliad*, where Priam and Achilles come to accept each other in their recognition of the primacy of family roles. That famous encounter from *Iliad* 24 has just been evoked through unusually close allusion in the visit that Snegiryov receives from Alyosha, a scene in which a grieving father, like Priam, receives one of those responsible. Those who received Hector's body in Troy are also represented: the distraught mother, Hecuba, finds a parallel in Snegiryov's "crazy weeping wife." Like the clairvoyant, doomed Cassandra, the crippled Nina is the only family member who sees clearly. The contrast of participants is as marked as in Homer: like the abject Priam, who has been rolling in the dung, Snegiryov is destitute, crazed, and sentimental. Though angelic rather than heroic, Alyosha, like Achilles, is the figure of youthful glory:

composed, sober, eloquent, emotionally generous. Snegiryov has lost a son, Alyosha a father, even as Priam and Achilles grieve for son and father, respectively. Both Achilles and Alyosha, though from the "enemy camp," come forth to acknowledge the harm that they have done to the grieving fathers. Both Ilyusha and Hector died fighting for the honor of their fathers. Consoling gestures deepen and complicate the character of both young men: the brutal, volatile, and selfish Achilles speaks compassionately and with almost philosophical detachment. Alyosha's gesture reminds us that, saintly as he is, he bears his own responsibility for Ilyusha's death, for he shares that part of Karamazov—the *kar*—that is (certainly in Dmitri) capable of destructiveness and baseness. In both scenes we see the anointed bodies of dead sons wrapped in shrouds and laid on coffin or couch. As Achilles finally bids Priam to put an end to grieving, so to Snegiryov does Alyosha offer the equivalent Christian solace: let us not weep for Ilyusha but cherish the memory of his presence when he was among us—and hope and live for the (positive) future. Achilles speaks in the resigned tones of one who has lived through it all: consider Peleus, my father, thought to be the luckiest of men. He married a goddess. But he had only a single son, who does not comfort his old age. With these words, he plays father to Priam.

Having experienced such a reversal of old and young with Snegiryov, Alyosha in the final scene assumes a paternal role with the twelve lads. In recommending food to the grieving survivors, he directly recalls Achilles' advice to Priam not to weep forever over Hector. Even Niobe, bereft of nine sons and nine daughters, took food and was comforted (*Iliad* 24.599–620). Such is Alyosha's final laughing advice to the twelve as well: "Don't be put out at our eating pancakes—it's a very old custom and there's something nice in that!" (p. 735). That funeral dinner is a Russian ritual that predates Christianity, a trace of the human origins of the eucharist itself.[24] The "unholy stone" (*poganyi kamen*—literally, "pagan, heathen") beside which the speech is given similarly combines Christian and pre-Christian associations. In this scene of foundation, it may represent the rock on which Jesus founded his church (Matthew 16:18) or the rock rolled from the tomb, the first sign of the victory over death.

Yet this pagan rock where Ilyusha wanted to be buried may also recall the only human landmark on the Trojan plain, the tomb of Ilus. The foundation myth of the death of Ilyusha unifies and invigorates this band even as the death of the founder Ilus stands behind Ilium.[25] As Ilus's tomb stands midway between the warring camps, so Ilyusha's tomb marks the center of Dostoevsky's moral geography. In this sense, Alyosha's boys have discovered the founders of Troy by becoming them. In the light of this final *Ilus-Ilyusha* etymology, it becomes less surprising that Zosima, as the locus of Christian authority, should have a name so reminiscent of Zeus; for Alyosha's memorialization of Ilyusha, his *Iliad*, though quintessentially Christian, presents itself as a prolegomenon to the opening note of the European tradition: the Homeric tale of wrath, of revenge, and of fathers and sons as they finally come to recognize each other. Alyosha's advice that there is nothing higher or more wholesome in life than a good memory renews that of Zosima, for of course Fyodor does not define the kind of father Alyosha is to be.

In this final moment, then, we have evocations equally of sacred and heroic poetry, of scripture and the *Iliad*, the horde and the twelve apostles. The gesture stands out all the more in an author who, unlike Gogol, is not given to such allusiveness. Both public and personal motives suggest themselves. Having taken on the role of prophet, Dostoevsky may have felt the pressures of tradition here at the end. Since *Dead Souls* attaches itself to the cycle of tales that started from Troy, *The Brothers Karamazov* cannot afford to do less, if only in its final moments, for it is by such linkages that the monumental tradition identifies itself. By ending his masterpiece with the "founders of Troy" allusively arrayed beside the founders of the Church, Dostoevsky invokes the secular and sacred traditions of the West from their origins and provides a genealogy for his work.

Another explanation comes from the formidably well-read Dostoevsky that one sees in his letters, a connoisseur of the classical texts that he does not invoke in his fiction. Two instances may be cited, separated by some fourteen years. The later one comes upon his release from prison in Siberia, before his return to civilian life. On February 22, 1854, he wrote asking his brother Mikhail to send books, namely, ancient and modern historians.[26] Here Vico leads the list. The Italian critic Attila Fáj has recently argued that the cyclical view of history in *The Brothers Karamazov* derives from Dostoevsky's reading of Vico's theories.[27] Fyodor and his sons are taken to represent the various phases of historical possibility as they all reassert themselves in the final decline: Fyodor represents prehistoric barbarism; Alyosha, the age of gods; Dmitri, the age of heroes; Ivan, the human period; Smerdyakov, renewed barbarism. If in fact Vico did fill the gap left by the now rejected Fourier and the utopians, then Dostoevsky, like Gogol with Dante, used Italian mysticism to free himself from French rationalism.

The typology of the brothers has, to be sure, been well explained in numerous other ways, and the Hesiodic-Platonic myth of the ages could have come to Dostoevsky through many channels other than Vico. Yet one can say that the final band of youths in a universe made newly poetic does come remarkably close to dramatizing the *ricorso* of Vico, the return to the rough, vital, and concretely sensual era that spawned the Achilleses, and later the Homers and the Dantes. Dostoevsky may in some measure have been led back to Homer by the same Neapolitan guide who later led Joyce.

The end of *The Brothers Karamazov* may constitute a *ricorso* of another and more personal sort. Amid the reflections on youth and age that end the tale, Dostoevsky obviously engages his own youth on many levels. Here, at the pinnacle of his achievement, we may perhaps see him confess to the formative impressions that inspired his ambitions and stayed with him throughout his life—to wit, his reverence for the two prophets of the West, Christ and Homer. To Mikhail, the eighteen-year-old Fyodor wrote, attributing an almost scriptural role to the *Iliad* very like that conferred on the *Odyssey* by Gogol in *Selected Passages*:

> As to Homer and Victor Hugo, it seems that you have deliberately chosen not to understand me. This is what I am saying: Homer (a legendary person who was perhaps incarnated and sent to us by God, as Christ was) can be compared only with Christ and not Goethe. Look through Homer, read the *Iliad* carefully and understand its meaning (admit, you haven't read it). In the *Iliad* Homer gave the whole ancient world the same organization in spiritual and earthly life that Christ gave to the new world.[28]

The Brothers Karamazov is not an epic. In formal and thematic terms, it continues that tradition much less than does *Dead Souls*. Rather, Dostoevsky created within the form of the novel a monumental surpassing of the novel that leaves off where the epic tradition takes up, as if—somehow—Chichikov, bounding directionless across the Russian steppe, were finally to draw near to a lofty city that might be Jerusalem, or might be windy Troy.

NOTES

Epic and Novel

1. "Èpopeya nashego vremeni est' roman," in V. G. Belinskii, "Razdelenie poèzii na rody i vidy," *Sobranie sochinenii v trekh tomakh* (Moscow, 1948), 2:38.

2. In a curiously Soviet interpretation of Russia's literary authority, the critic L. F. Ershov disputes all claims that modernist literature can in any way embody the epic tradition. Insisting that classical epics reconstitute the moment of unity in a nation's history such as cannot be achieved in bourgeois society, this orthodox Marxist concludes that contemporary Western literature is fundamentally incapable of producing epic novels. "However," Ershov continues, "to any unbiased observer who can recall but three literary works—*Taras Bulba*, *War and Peace*, and *The Quiet Don*—it is clear that only in Russia have the lessons of universal, primarily Greek and Latin epic art been consistently and organically mastered." L. F. Ershov, "Traditsii M. Sholokhova i roman-èpopeya v slavyanskikh stranakh," *Acta Litteraria Academiae Scientiarum Hungaricae* 28, nos. 3–4 (1986): 318.

3. Boris Eikhenbaum, *Tolstoi in the Sixties*, trans. Duffield White (Ann Arbor, Mich.: Ardis, 1982), 227. Originally published as *Lev Tolstoi, Kniga Vtoraya* (Leningrad, 1930).

4. F. T. Griffiths and S. J. Rabinowitz, "Tolstoy and Homer," *Comparative Literature* 35 (1983): 97–125.

5. Boris Pasternak, *Doctor Zhivago*, prose trans. Max Hayward and Manya Harari, poetic trans. Bernard Guerney (New York: Pantheon, 1958; rpt. New York: Bantam, 1985), 43. See F. T. Griffiths and S. J. Rabinowitz, "*Doctor Zhivago* and the Tradition of National Epic," *Comparative Literature* 32 (1980): 63–79.

6. For some stimulating thoughts on Gogol's influence particularly on Dostoevsky's early works, see Donald Fanger, *Dostoevsky and Romantic Realism* (Cambridge, Mass.: Harvard University Press, 1965), as well as Fanger's "Influence and Tradition in the Russian Novel," *The Russian Novel from Pushkin to Pasternak*, ed. John Garrard (New Haven and London: Yale University Press, 1983), 29–

50, and in general Priscilla Meyer and Stephen Rudy, eds., *Dostoevsky and Gogol* (Ann Arbor, Mich.: Ardis, 1979).

7. The most comprehensive examination of Gogol's indebtedness to the European literary tradition is Anna Yelistratova, *Nikolai Gogol and the West European Novel*, trans. Christopher English (Moscow: Raduga Publishers, 1984). She discusses no influence earlier than the "epic novel" (Cervantes, Sterne, Fielding, et al.).

8. E. M. W. Tillyard, *The Epic Strain in the English Novel* (London: Chatto and Windus, 1958), 16.

9. Quoted in Viktor Afanasev, ed., *N. Gnedich, Stikhotvoreniya i poèmy* (Moscow, 1984), 7.

10. Manuscript 423, Sankt-Peterburgskaya Dukhovnaya Akademiya, an untitled grammatical thesis published in M. N. Smenkovskii, *Brat'ia Likhudy* (St. Petersbrug, 1899), ix; the translation is that of Richard Burgi, *A History of the Russian Hexameter* (Hamden, Conn.: The Shoe String Press, 1954), 11.

11. Quoted in A. N. Egunov, "Lomonosov-perevodchik Gomera," in *Literaturnoe tvorchestvo M. V. Lomonosova* (Moscow-Leningrad, 1962), 215.

12. Leo Tolstoy, *"What Is Art?" and "Essays on Art,"* trans. Aylmer Maude (London: Oxford University Press, 1929), 178. See, in general, Chauncey E. Finch, "Tolstoy as a Student of the Classics," *Classical Journal* 47 (1952): 205–10. The comparison of Homer to the Old Testament and to Christ was a commonplace already in the eighteenth century; see Kirsti Simonsuuri, *Homer's Original Genius: Eighteenth-century Notions of the Early Greek Epic (1688–1798)* (Cambridge: Cambridge University Press, 1979), 145–52.

13. Fyodor Dostoevsky, letter to M. M. Dostoevsky, January 1, 1840, in F. M. Dostoevskii, *Polnoe sobranie sochinenii v 30 tomakh*, vol. 28, pt. 1 (Leningrad: Nauka, 1985), 69.

14. Carl Proffer, *The Simile and Gogol's Dead Souls* (The Hague: Mouton, 1967), 166–82.

15. Walter Benjamin, "The Storyteller," in *Illuminations*, ed. Hannah Arendt, trans. Harry Zohn (New York: Schocken Books, 1969), 97.

16. Serviceable surveys of these characteristics can still be found in Cecil M. Bowra, *From Virgil to Milton* (London: Macmillan and Co., 1945), 1–32; E. M. W. Tillyard, *The English Epic and Its Background* (New York: Oxford University Press, 1954), 4–13; Thomas M. Greene, *The Descent from Heaven* (New Haven and London: Yale

University Press, 1963), 8–25; and Daniel Madelénat, *L'Epopée* (Paris: Presses universitaires de France, 1986), 17–78.

17. E. M. W. Tillyard, *Epic Strain;* F. R. Leavis, *The Great Tradition: George Eliot, Henry James, Joseph Conrad* (London: Chatto and Windus, 1950); Frank Kermode, *The Classic: Literary Images of Permanence and Change* (New York: Viking, 1975).

18. Alessandro Manzoni, *On the Historical Novel,* trans. Sandra Bermann (Lincoln and London: University of Nebraska Press, 1984), 103. Originally published as *Del romanzo storico* (Milan, 1845).

19. G. W. F. Hegel, *The Philosophy of Fine Art,* trans. F. P. B. Osmaston (London: G. Bell and Sons, 1920), 4:133.

20. William A. Butler, in an unsigned review in the Washington, D.C., *National Intelligencer,* December 16, 1851, excerpted in *Melville: The Critical Heritage,* ed. Watson G. Branch (London and Boston: Routledge and Kegan Paul, 1974), 283.

21. See, in general, Severin Koster, *Antike Epostheorien,* Palingenesia, vol. 5 (Wiesbaden: Franz Steiner Verlag, 1970).

22. That the epic may be written in prose as well as verse is an article of faith already for Cervantes's Canon of Toledo in *Don Quixote,* pt. 1, chap. 47.

23. See Charles Rowan Beye, *Epic and Romance in the* Argonautica *of Apollonius,* Literary Structures (Carbondale and Edwardsville: University of Southern Illinois Press, 1982).

24. On the current possibilities for epic, including film, see "Forms of Modern Epic" in Paul Merchant, *The Epic,* The Critical Idiom, vol. 17 (London: Methuen and Company, 1971; rpt. 1979), 71–94, an engaging brief introduction to the whole epic tradition.

25. On *Paradise Lost* as a textbook for montage and audiovisual relationships, see Sergei M. Eisenstein, *The Film Sense,* trans. and ed. Jay Leyda (New York: Harcourt, Brace and Company, 1942), 58–62.

26. A comprehensive survey of the American and European historical dramas in this category can be found in Derek Elley, *The Epic Film: Myth and History* (London: Routledge and Kegan Paul, 1984).

27. See especially the excerpts from "Der Dreigroschenprozess," sections III (1) and (6) translated in Bertolt Brecht, *Brecht on Theater: The Development of an Aesthetic,* trans. John Willet (London and New York: Harcourt, Brace and World, 1964; rpt. 1984), 47–51.

28. See the analysis of Robert Stam, *Reflexivity in Film and Literature from Don Quixote to Jean-Luc Godard.* Studies in Cinema, vol. 31 (Ann Arbor, Mich.: UMI Research Press, 1985), 21–22.

29. Jean-Luc Godard, *Godard on Godard*, trans. Tom Milne, ed. Jean Narboni and Tom Milne (New York and London: Viking, 1972; rpt., New York: Da Capo Press, 1986), 201. Originally published as *Jean-Luc Godard par Jean-Luc Godard* (Paris: B. Belfond, 1968).

30. To trace but one recent swing from dismantling to synthesis (and Left to Right), the antinarrative techniques of the French New Wave proved useful in the revival of the American film industry after 1967. The most extravagant and profitable "screen epics" in film history (for example, the *Star Wars* and Indiana Jones trilogies) employ overt allusiveness, stylization of gesture, and cartoonlike externality that (*pace* Brecht and Godard) facilitate escapism. On the first decade of this development, see Robert Ray, *A Certain Tendency of the Hollywood Cinema, 1930–1980* (Princeton, N.J.: Princeton University Press, 1985), 272ff.

31. On Aristotle's use of Homer in the *Poetics*, see, in particular, Stephen Halliwell, *Aristotle's* Poetics (Chapel Hill: University of North Carolina Press, 1986), 253–66.

32. See, in general, Paul A. Olson, "The Epic and Great Plains Literature: Rølvaag, Cather, and Neihardt," *Prairie Schooner* 55 (1981): 263–85. The scene may also recall Goethe's reading the *Odyssey* and discovering the *Urmensch* in Sicily.

33. One of the earliest traces of this device is found in Thucydides. "We shall need no Homer to sing our praises," proclaims Pericles to the Athenians in his funeral oration (2.51), testifying both to the doomed self-assurance of imperial Athens and, at another level, to Thucydides' own claims as the writer of another great book about another great war (a greater war, he argues, than the Trojan).

34. Alastair Fowler, "The Life and Death of Literary Forms," in *New Directions in Literary History*, ed. Ralph Cohen (Baltimore: The Johns Hopkins University Press, 1974), 87.

35. The *Nachleben* of Homer and Virgil can be traced throughout the Renaissance by reading their respective entries in the indices to Ernst Robert Curtius, *European Literature and the Latin Middle Ages*, trans. Willard R. Trask, Bollingen Series 36 (Princeton, N.J.: Princeton University Press, 1953), and R. R. Bolgar, *The Classical Heritage and Its Beneficiaries* (Cambridge: Cambridge University Press, 1954). On Virgil, see Domenico Comparetti, *Vergil in the Middle Ages*, trans. E. F. M. Benecke (London and New York, 1895). Simonsuuri summarizes Homer's role in the earlier centuries (*Homer's Original Genius*, 3–16) before his survey of the eighteenth century.

36. Georg Lukács, *The Theory of the Novel,* trans. Anna Bostock (Cambridge, Mass.: MIT Press, 1971). Originally published as *Die Theorie des Romans* (Berlin: P. Cassirer, 1920). A helpful introduction to these theories is provided by Michel Aucouturier, "The Theory of the Novel in Russia in the 1930s: Lukács and Bakhtin," in *The Russian Novel from Pushkin to Pasternak,* ed. John Garrard (New Haven and London: Yale University Press, 1983), 227–40.

37. Mikhail M. Bakhtin, "Epic and Novel" and "From the Prehistory of Novelistic Discourse," in his *The Dialogic Imagination,* ed. Michael Holquist, trans. Caryl Emerson and Michael Holquist (Austin: University of Texas Press, 1981), 3–83.

38. As a spokesman for his age, Homer is in considerable decline among classicists. Archeologists no longer feel compelled to heed him at all. Already twenty-five years ago Emily Vermeule, in introducing her important *Greece in the Bronze Age* (Chicago and London: The University of Chicago Press, 1964), wrote, "Homer has been rejected as evidence, with a pang" (p. x).

39. Lukács, *Theory of the Novel,* 30.

40. How much alienation we may see in Achilles and how much we should suspect modern biases in doing so remains the slipperiest of Homeric questions. For the state of the controversy, see James M. Redfield, *Nature and Culture in the* Iliad: *The Tragedy of Hector* (Chicago and London: The University of Chicago Press, 1975), 3–29.

41. This position is argued concisely by Adam Parry, "The Language of Achilles," *Transactions and Proceedings of the American Philological Association* 87 (1956): 1–7, reprinted in *The Language and Background of Homer: Some Recent Studies and Controversies,* ed. Geoffrey S. Kirk (Cambridge: Heffer; New York: Barnes and Noble, 1964), 48–54, and in *Homer,* ed. Harold Bloom, Modern Critical Views (New York: Chelsea House Publishers, 1986), 109–13. For a wider development of this approach, see Cedric H. Whitman, *Homer and the Homeric Tradition* (Cambridge, Mass.: Harvard University Press, 1958). See, most recently, Stephen A. Nimis, *Narrative Semiotics in the Epic Tradition: The Simile* (Bloomington and Indianapolis: Indiana University Press, 1987), 63–73.

42. For the fullest and most recent interpretation of that literary relationship, see Pietro Pucci, *Odysseus Polutropos: Intertextual Readings in the* Odyssey *and the* Iliad (Ithaca and London: Cornell University Press, 1987).

43. Thomas Babington Macaulay, *Critical and Historical Essays Contributed to the Edinburgh Review* (London: Longmans, Green,

and Company, 1909), 1:13, quoted by Donal M. Foerster in *The Fortunes of Epic Poetry: A Study in English and American Criticism 1750-1950* (Washington, D.C.: Catholic University Press, 1962), 149.

44. Geoffrey S. Kirk, *The Songs of Homer* (Cambridge: Cambridge University Press, 1962), 280. See, in general, 271–300.

45. Nikolai V. Gogol, *Selected Passages from Correspondence with Friends*, trans. Jesse Zeldin (Nashville, Tenn.: Vanderbilt University Press, 1969), 248. When necessary, we have altered Zeldin's translation to provide more accuracy.

46. Gary Saul Morson, *Hidden in Plain View: Narrative and Creative Potentials in* War and Peace (Stanford, Calif.: Stanford University Press, 1987).

47. Julia Kristeva, *Sēmeiōtikē: recherches pour une sémanalyse*, Collection "Tel Quel" (Paris: Editions du Seuil, 1969), 163.

48. Bakhtin, "Epic and Novel," 36.

49. E. L. Bowie, "The Greek Novel," in *The Cambridge History of Classical Literature*, vol. 1, *Greek Literature*, ed. P. E. Easterling and B. M. W. Knox (Cambridge: Cambridge University Press, 1985; rpt. 1987), 688.

50. Bakhtin discusses the influence of the Bible, but not its creation (see "From the History of Novelistic Discourse," 69–71). Writing before this essay was published, Erich Auerbach, in *Mimesis*, contrasted the externality of Homeric characterization with a more mixed and inward-looking style first exemplified in Genesis. Auerbach's characterization of Homeric style has largely been dismissed by classicists; see, for example, Jasper Griffin, *Homer on Life and Death* (Oxford: Clarendon Press, 1980; rpt., 1983), 50–80 (earlier critiques cited, p. 70, n. 37). On Bakhtin and Auerbach, see Tzvetan Todorov, *Mikhail Bakhtin: The Dialogical Principle*, trans. Wlad Godzich, Theory and History of Literature, vol. 13 (Minneapolis: University of Minnesota Press, 1980), 89–90. Originally published as *Mikhaïl Bakhtine: le principe dialogique* (Paris: Editions du Seuil, 1981).

51. Even three decades ago Hermann Fränkel, a scholar of Auerbach's generation and similarly a proponent of *Geistesgeschichte*, could describe what in Bakhtin's terms seems to be a dialogical quality in Homer: "The restraint which the epic poet imposes upon himself is set aside in the numerous speeches which he weaves into his work. Only so long as the singer is reporting events does he remain a mere shadow, discreet and neutral. . . . In general the speeches are freer and richer; their style and their mode and course of thought are more

modern than is narrative. In the speeches we find quite often ideas, reflections, relationships, in contradiction to those upon which the narrative and action rest. It is as if forces held in check had here broken out with elemental strength." *Early Greek Poetry and Philosophy*, trans. Moses Hadas and James Willis (New York and London: Harcourt Brace Jovanovich, 1975), 39–40. Originally published as *Dichtung und Philosophie des frühen Griechentums* (Munich: C. H. Beck'sche Verlagsbuchhandlung, 1962).

52. That it was the very marginality of Ionia which enabled the Homeric definition of "Greekness" is a traditional speculation elegantly formulated by E. M. W. Tillyard, *English Epic*, 36–39.

53. Along with Auerbach, see, for example, the readings of Robert Alter, *The Art of Biblical Narrative* (New York: Basic Books, 1981).

54. On the nature of the performances that lie behind the Homeric texts, see Eric A. Havelock, *Preface to Plato* (Cambridge, Mass.: Harvard University Press, and Oxford: Basil Blackwell, 1963; rpt., New York: Bantam, 1982), 145–64; Joseph Russo and Bennett Simon, "Homeric Psychology and the Oral Epic Tradition," *Journal of the History of Ideas* 29 (1968): 485–98; and Bennett Simon, *Mind and Madness in Ancient Greece: The Classical Roots of Modern Psychology* (Ithaca and London: Cornell University Press, 1978), 78–88.

55. Harold Bloom, *A Map of Misreading* (New York: Oxford University Press, 1975), 138. Milton's inversion of time may derive from the scene in the *Aeneid* (8.626–728) where the baffled Aeneas looks on a divine shield summarizing the history of a Rome that has not yet been founded. Leo Bersani, "Against *Ulysses*," *Raritan* 8, no. 2 (Fall 1988): 21, observes a similar absorption and reconstitution of canon in *Ulysses:* "The Joycean intertext rescues Western literature from the deconstructive effects of the intertext itself. The parodistic replays of Homer, Shakespeare, and Flaubert—not to speak of all the authors "quoted" in "Oxen of the Sun"—are neither subversive of nor indifferent to the fact of cultural inheritance; rather, Joyce relocates the items of that inheritance with *Ulysses* as both their center and belated origin."

56. On Dante's restaging of the tradition, see the section "Epic Resolution" in Teodolinda Barolini, *Dante's Poets: Textuality and Truth in the* Comedy (Princeton, N.J.: Princeton University Press, 1984), 188–296.

57. On Ovid and epic, see Brooks Otis, *Ovid as an Epic Poet* (Cambridge: Cambridge University Press, 1966; 2d ed., 1970) and

Robert Coleman's review, "Ovid and the Anti-Epic," *Classical Review* n.s. 17 (1967): 46–51.

58. See Louis L. Martz, *Poet of Exile: A Study of Milton's Poetry* (New Haven and London: Yale University Press, 1980), and Richard J. DuRocher, *Milton and Ovid* (Ithaca and London: Cornell University Press, 1985), who usefully survey work on countergenre.

59. For an astute appreciation of the interplay of the high and low mimetic modes in heroic literature, see George deForest Lord, *Heroic Mockery: Variations on Epic Themes from Homer to Joyce* (Newark, Del.: University of Delaware Press, 1977).

60. Ralph Cohen argues that the basis of genres in the eighteenth century was a hierarchy in which the lower forms tended to inclusion in the higher (for example, epigram into satire, sonnet into drama). As the highest form, epic was the most inclusive. See "On the Interrelations of Eighteenth-Century Literary Forms," in *New Approaches to Eighteenth-Century Literature*, ed. Phillip Harth (New York and London: Columbia University Press, 1974), 33–78.

61. In Goethe's 1797 essay (published in 1827 and cosigned by Schiller) "Über epische und dramatische Dichtung," in *Goethes Werke*, ed. Erich Trunz, Hamburger Ausgabe in 14 Bänden, vol. 12 (12th ed., 1981), 249–51.

62. Goethe locates the distinction in the different modes of performing, not writing, epic and tragedy, that is, between the rhapsode's impersonal narration of past events and the mime's reenactment. Later work on oral poetry has largely discredited this distinction (see above, nn. 50 and 54). More than half of both the *Iliad* and the *Odyssey* consists of highly performable speeches.

In his critique of Bakhtin's failure ever to define or limit the category of "novel," Todorov (*Mikhail Bakhtin*, 89–90) discusses this transformation of Goethe's antithesis and notes that Plato would class both epic and novel as *diēgēsis*, as Bakhtin himself tends to do in his later writings.

63. This possibility has been explored most fully by Gregory Nagy, *The Best of the Achaeans* (Baltimore and London: The Johns Hopkins University Press, 1979; rpt., 1981).

64. Lukács, *Theory of the Novel*, 82. John Freccero uses Lukács's observation as the basis for a reading of *Inferno* 26. See "Dante's Ulysses: From Epic to Novel," in *Concepts of the Hero in the Middle Ages and the Renaissance*, ed. Norman T. Burns and Christopher J. Reagan (Albany: SUNY Press, 1975), 101–19; reprinted in John

Freccero, *Dante: The Poetics of Conversion*, ed. and intro. Rachel Jacoff (Cambridge, Mass.: Harvard University Press, 1986), 136–51.

Gogol in Rome

1. The fullest account of Gogol's sojourn is Sigrid Richter's Hamburg University dissertation, "Rom und Gogol': Gogol's Romerlebnis und sein Fragment 'Rim'" (1964).

2. See Eliza Marian Butler, *The Tyranny of Greece over Germany* (Cambridge: Cambridge University Press, 1935; rpt., Boston: Beacon Press, 1958).

3. For some interesting thoughts on this subject, as well as on Gogol's narrative art in general, see Hugh McLean, "Gogol and the Whirling Telescope," in *Russia: Essays in History and Literature*, ed. G. Lyman and M. Legters (Leiden: Brill, 1972), 79–99.

4. N. V. Gogol, *Sobranie sochinenii v semi tomakh* (Moscow, 1966–67), 7:177.

5. N. V. Gogol, *Polnoe sobranie sochinenii* (Moscow, 1937–52), 11:115. For a brief survey of his classical background, see Chauncey E. Finch, "Classical Influence on N. V. Gogol," *Classical Journal* 48 (1953): 291–96.

6. Quoted by V. V. Gippius in *Gogol*, ed. and trans. Robert A. Maguire (Ann Arbor, Mich.: Ardis, 1981), 97.

7. P. V. Annenkov, "N. V. Gogol' v Rime letom 1841 goda," in *Gogol' v vospominaniyakh sovremennikov*, ed. S. Mashinskii (Moscow, 1952), 273. On June 3, 1837, Gogol wrote to his friend N. Y. Prokopovich about the Italian sounds of Tasso and Dante (*Polnoe sobranie sochinenii*, 11:102). On August 10, 1839, he wrote to S. P. Shevyrev to thank and heartily praise him for his translation of Dante (ibid., 11:247). It is unknown precisely when Gogol first read Dante, but the noted scholar F. C. Driessen finds a parallel between *Inferno* 32 and 33 and Gogol's early story "A Terrible Vengeance" (1831). See Driessen, *Gogol as Short Story Writer* (The Hague: Mouton, 1965), 109. By March 15, 1839, he had sufficient Italian to write a long letter to M. P. Balabina. For a compilation of all attributed evidence of Gogol's responses to Dante, see A. A. Asoyan, "Zametki o dantovskikh motivakh u Belinskogo i Gogolya," in *Dantovskie Chteniya 1985* (Moscow: Nauka, 1985), 104–19.

8. N. V. Gogol, *"The Overcoat" and Other Tales of Good and Evil*, trans. David Magarshack (New York: W. W. Norton and Company, 1965), 130.

9. E.-M. de Vogüé, *The Russian Novel* (London: Chapman and Hall, 1913), see esp. 129 and 141. Originally published as *Le Roman russe* (Paris, 1880).

10. Gogol himself eschewed uncomplicated typologies and revealed his bewilderment over distinguishing what, precisely, he was creating, when he insisted that "the thing over which I am sitting and working [*Dead Souls*]...is not like a tale or a novel" (*Polnoe sobranie sochinenii*, 11:77). Using similar language, Tolstoy also expressed bewilderment over trying to classify *War and Peace* when he claimed that "this work of mine is not a tale...it cannot be called a novel." (Leo Tolstoy, "Draft for an Introduction," in *War and Peace*, trans. George Gibian [New York: W. W. Norton and Company, 1966], 1363).

"TARAS BULBA"

11. On these similes and other Homeric devices in "Taras Bulba" see Carl Proffer, *The Simile and Gogol's* Dead Souls (The Hague: Mouton, 1967), 166–82.

12. The ramifying complexity of this tradition is traced from Homer to Milton by Stephen A. Nimis, *Narrative Semiotics in the Epic Tradition: The Simile* (Bloomington and Indianapolis: Indiana University Press, 1987).

13. Translations of "Taras Bulba," "A Terrible Vengeance," and "Viy" are by Christopher English and appear in *Nikolai Gogol: A Selection* (Moscow: Progress Publishers, 1981).

14. The passage in question reads in Russian: "Nemalaya reka Dnestr, i mnogo na nei zavod'ev, rechnykh gustykh kamnei, otmelei i glubokodonnykh mest; blestit rechnoe zerkalo, oglashennoe zvonkim yachan'em lebedei, i gordyi *gogol'* bystro nesetsya po nem..." (our italics).

15. That Gogol himself found the work flawed is seen in his confession to Zhukovsky that "all of the shortcomings that 'Taras Bulba' and 'Old World Landowners' abound in were totally unnoticeable to everyone except you, me, and Pushkin." N. V. Gogol, letter to V. A. Zhukovsky, April 6, 1837, in *Polnoe sobranie sochinenii*, 11:98.

16. Renato Poggioli, "Gogol's 'Old-Fashioned Landowners': An Inverted Eclogue," *Indiana Slavic Studies* 3 (1963): 54–72.

17. "Old World Landowners" in Nikolai V. Gogol, *Mirgorod*, trans. David Magarshack (New York: Noonday, 1962), 18.

18. The addition of gluttony to Ovid's charming tale about the old couple (*Met.* 8.618–724) might well have been inspired by the following tale of Erysichthon (8.738–876), whose impiety was punished by a voraciousness climaxing in autocannibalism.

19. Further illumination of this point can be found in Richard Peace, *The Enigma of Gogol* (Cambridge: Cambridge University Press, 1981), 87.

20. Proffer, *The Simile*, 183–200.

21. Gogol admitted to the "safe" nationalist politics of "Taras Bulba" when he asked Zhukovsky: "Find the occasion and the means somehow to show the Czar my tales 'Old World Landowners' and 'Taras Bulba.' These are the two fortunate pieces that have totally satisfied all tastes and all temperaments" (*Polnoe sobranie sochinenii*, 11:337).

"ROME"

22. Richter, "Rom und Gogol': Gogol's Romerlebnis und sein Fragment 'Rim'," 126–44.

23. T. Baroti, "Traditsiya Dante i povest' Gogolya 'Rim,'" *Studia Slavica Hungarica* 29 (1983): 171–83.

24. Annunziata appears first on a wagon in Carnival, as Beatrice does in the Procession of the Host (*Purg.* 30). So it will be later with the redemptive Ulinka, in *Dead Souls*, Part Two.

25. In one of the most informative analyses of "Rome," Louis Pedrotti writes, "Although Gogol later asserted that the views of his anonymous prince should not be confused with his own, there is little doubt that there are strong autobiographical elements in the story." For further treatment of this issue, and many others, see Louis Pedrotti, "The Architecture of Love in Gogol's *Rome*," *California Slavic Studies* 6 (1971): 17–27.

26. Daria Borghese, *Gogol a Roma* (Florence: Sansoni, n.d.), 57, argues that Gogol converted the Italian baroque style into Russian: "Questo linguaggio è un vero prodigio di stile barocco italiano interpretato in lingua russa." Does this style not constitute a surface reflection of the larger ambition of transferring Rome's spiritual authority to its final home, Russia?

27. See Richter, "Rom und Gogol'," 24–37. For an enlightening discussion of Gogol's attraction to Rome and Catholicism, see Victor Erlich, *Gogol* (New Haven and London: Yale University Press, 1969), esp. 158–65.

28. Gogol, *Sobranie sochinenii v semi tomakh* (Moscow, 1966–67), 3:247. The translation is our own.

29. Gogol, *Polnoe sobranie sochinenii,* 8:478–79. Only a sketch of Gogol's work remains. In it the author defines and compares several literary genres. The section that we quote, "malaya èpopeya," comes closest to his realization of *Dead Souls,* especially when Gogol writes, "In the modern era there originated a kind of narrative work that constitutes, as it were, a cross between a novel and an epic, the hero of which, although a private and unnoteworthy character, is significant nevertheless for the observer of human souls."

30. Translations are by Bernard Guilbert Guerney, *Chichikov's Journeys: or, Home Life in Old Russia* (New York: The Readers Club, 1942). We have corrected any deficiencies against the original.

31. See the discussion of Donald Fanger, *The Creation of Nikolai Gogol* (Cambridge, Mass.: Harvard University Press, 1979), 170.

32. This image is balanced at the very end of chapter 11, where Chichikov's damnation is figured similarly: "And perhaps, as in this very Chichikov, the passion that is drawing him on is not of his choosing, and in his chill existence is contained that which will cast man down into the dust and on his knees before the wisdom of the heavens" (p. 229).

33. This is George Reavey's translation (Nikolai V. Gogol, *Dead Souls* [New York: W. W. Norton, 1971], 273), which contrasts with Guerney's rendition ("So is he still vegetating in this world?"). Here the root *zyab* does indeed indicate vegetation, but on occasion it also suggests coldness or chilliness. Perhaps Gogol intended this association as well.

34. The earliest extended critical discussion of the relationship—real and proposed—between *Dead Souls* and *The Divine Comedy* is found in A. Veselovskii, " 'Mertvye Dushi': Glava iz ètiuda o Gogole," *Vestnik Evropy* 3 (1891): 68–102, esp. 89–91. See, most recently, Yurii Mann, *Poètika Gogolya* (Moscow: Khudozhestvennaya Literatura, 1978), esp. 339–52; A. A. Asoyan, "Zametki o dantovskikh motivakh u Belinskogo i Gogolya," 104–19; and Marianne Shapiro, "Gogol and Dante," *Modern Language Studies* 17, no. 2 (Spring 1987): 37–54; reprinted in Michael and Marianne Shapiro, *Figuration in Verbal Art* (Princeton, N.J.: Princeton University Press, 1988), 191–211.

35. The allusion is discussed by Shapiro, "Gogol and Dante," 46–48 [=*Figuration*, 204–6]. Her astute comparison of Dante's shades and Gogol's landowners as symbol systems essentially ends with the visit to Pliushkin. We differ in seeing Gogol's allegory, like Dante's, as also dynamic. Pliushkin's garden, like that of the suicides, is not only a climactic symbol but the threshold of a yet steeper descent. While character does not develop in the landowners any more than among the shades, the concept of character does, for, as we shall argue, certain nimble human entities (Dante-pilgrim, Gogol's narrator) do escape these deadening realms.

36. The image recurs in Chichikov's biography: "Anew he withdrew into himself, like a hedgehog . . ." (p. 225). In both cases Gogol uses the verb *s"ezhit'sya*, which means to shrivel or shrink, and which contains the word for hedgehog, *ezh*.

37. Fanger, *Creation of Nikolai Gogol*, 189.

38. Shapiro, "Gogol and Dante," 45–48 [= *Figuration* 203–7].

39. Fanger notes this quality of Gogol's novel when he claims that "If *Dead Souls* seems colder in its brilliance than any of the previous writings, it is because there alone the values of childhood and free fantasy have virtually no place. An informing nostalgia for the past had yielded to an anxious concern for the future" (*Creation of Nikolai Gogol*, 246).

40. Fanger, ibid., 174.

41. See Simon Karlinsky, *The Sexual Labyrinth of Nikolai Gogol* (Cambridge, Mass.: Harvard University Press, 1976), 239.

DEAD SOULS, PART TWO

42. Gogol's expression is *koptitel' neba*, an idiom that means to idle one's life away, to live aimlessly. Reavey renders the phrase as "sky-gazer," thereby including the sense of *nebo*, which means sky or heavens. The literal meaning of the phrase is "to besmirch the sky with soot."

43. Rosette C. Lamont, "Joseph Brodsky: A Poet's Classroom," *The Massachusetts Review* 15, no. 4 (Autumn 1974): 553–77.

44. Further evidence supporting the autobiographical relationship between Gogol and Tentetnikov may be found in the author's letter to Zhukovsky of December 29, 1847, in which he also uses the expression "bol'shoe sochinenie," a great or major work. See *Sobranie sochinenii v semi tomakh*, 7:361.

45. See Gippius, *Gogol*, 170.

46. See ibid., 175.

47. Marianne Shapiro sees instead a scheme based on the Gregorian seven cardinal vices distributed throughout all of Purgatory: "Each character newly presented in this volume adheres more clearly than his counterpart in the first to a specific vice by which he is defined. Tentetnikov (whose name is based on *ten'*, 'shadow, shade'), has a biography but is particularized for sloth, the grounding sin which together with greed (materiality) guarantees petrification. Kostanzhoglo virtually stands for anger; General Betrishchev, for pride; Khlobuyev for prodigality, Koshkarev, for gluttony. As in Dante's *Purgatory*, sloth (*acedia*) is the preambular vice that introduces the others." "Gogol and Dante," 48 [= *Figuration*, 207].

48. Quoted in P. V. Annenkov, "N. V. Gogol' v Rime letom 1841 goda," in *Gogol' v vospominaniyakh sovremennikov*, ed. S. Mashinskii (Moscow, 1952), 283.

49. Kostonzhoglo and Skudronzhoglo are the same person.

SELECTED PASSAGES FROM CORRESPONDENCE WITH FRIENDS

50. A recent student of Gogol's last published work, Jesse Zeldin, argues that it represents the ideas upon which the author proposed to base at least the second part of his trilogy, if not the third as well, and that it "points the way to a regeneration of the 'dead souls' whom he finds in Part One, in much the way that Dante's *Purgatorio* shows the way of salvation for sinners—not a contradiction of *Inferno*, but a part of the same structure in which *Inferno*, *Purgatorio*, and *Paradiso* all have a definite place." Introduction to his translation of Gogol's *Selected Passages from Correspondence with Friends*, xv. Andrei Sinyavskii (Abram Terz) makes some excellent comments on this topic in his book *V teni Gogolya* (London: Collins, 1975), esp. 204–7.

51. Translations are by Zeldin, *Selected Passages*.

52. James M. Holquist, "The Burden of Prophecy: Gogol's Conception of Russia," *Review of National Literatures* 3, no. 1 (Spring 1972): 41.

53. Holquist (ibid., 51) extends the list of possible messianic or prophetic models recalled in Gogol's letters to include John the Baptist and, perhaps, Christ himself.

54. Quoted by Terz, *V teni Gogolya*, 295.

55. Fanger, *Creation of Nikolai Gogol*, 214.

56. "...after having read the whole book [Part One], it seems exactly as though he [the reader] were emerging from some stifling cellar into God's light." Gogol, *Selected Passages*, 104.

57. One wonders, of course, how Pushkin would have reacted to his newly evangelical friend. Gogol has dealt with this problem retroactively in chapter 14, "On the Theater," by refuting imputations of deism to Pushkin and by rehabilitating him as a Christian. Even Pushkin's 1830 "When out of sport or idle boredom" becomes Christian with the omission of its first stanza (pp. 82–83). One is reminded of the posthumous conversion that Dante wished for Virgil.

58. *Sobranie sochinenii v semi tomakh*, 7:427.

59. Letter of May 1, 1881, quoted in N. N. Gusev, *Letopis' zhizni i tvorchestva L'va Nikolaevicha Tolstogo* (Moscow, 1958), 535.

60. Letter of July 13 to A. O. Smirnova in *Polnoe sobranie sochinenii*, 12:504.

61. André Gide, *Dostoevsky* (New York: New Directions, 1961), 50. Originally published as *Dostoïevsky: articles et causeries* (Paris: Plon, 1923).

Dostoevsky's The Brothers Karamazov

1. Letter to A. N. Maykov, Dresden, March 25, 1870, in Fyodor M. Dostoevsky, *The Brothers Karamazov*, trans. Constance Garnett and Ralph Matlaw, ed. Ralph Matlaw (New York: W. W. Norton and Company, 1976), 752–53.

2. Anna Dostoevsky, *Dostoevsky-Reminiscences*, trans. and ed. Beatrice Stillman (New York: Liveright, 1975), 158. Originally published as *Vospominaniya* (Moscow, 1925).

3. Letter to N. N. Strakhov, December 2, 1870, in *F. M. Dostoevskii-Pisma*, ed. A. S. Dolinin (Moscow-Leningrad, 1930), 2:298.

4. Ibid., 290. In his famous letter to Zhukovsky of December 29, 1847, Gogol also distinguishes between poet and artist, implying that the continuation of *Dead Souls* required more the talents of a poet than of an artist: "But in general one should focus not on *censuring* others but on *contemplating* one's own self. If the creation of the poet does not contain within it this quality, then it is merely... the fruit of the temporary state of the artist." See N. V. Gogol, *Sobranie sochinenii v semi tomakh* (Moscow, 1966–67), 7:363.

5. Donald Fanger, "Influence and Tradition in the Russian Novel," in John Garrard, ed., *The Russian Novel from Pushkin to Pasternak* (New Haven and London: Yale University Press, 1983), 48.

6. For a discussion of *The Brothers Karamazov* as an exposition of the "main novel," see Maximilian Braun, *"The Brothers Karamazov* as an Expository Novel," *Canadian-American Slavic Studies* 6 (1972): 199–208. For a contrary opinion that interprets the "projected" continuation to the novel as a literary device of Dostoevsky's narrator, see Robert Belknap, *The Structure of* The Brothers Karamazov (The Hague: Mouton, 1967; rpt., Evanston, Ill.: Northwestern University Press, 1989), esp. 107–8.

7. See Pavel M. Bitsilli, "Pochemu Dostoevskii ne napisal *Zhitie velikogo greshnika,"* in *O Dostoevskom. Sbornik statei,* ed. A. L. Bem (Paris: AMGA Editions, 1986), 149–54.

8. Cited by Beatrice Stillman in her notes to Anna Dostoevsky, *Dostoevsky-Reminiscences,* 410.

9. Fanger, "Influence and Tradition," 47.

10. All citations from the text are from the Garnett-Matlaw translation of the Norton Critical Edition (above, n. 1).

11. Given the importance of symbolic foreshadowing in *The Brothers Karamazov,* it is probably not accidental that Gogol's earliest short stories constitute Smerdyakov's first and ostensibly exclusive experience in reading fiction. Though filled with lovely scenes, exuberant village life, and local Ukrainian color, the tales are permeated with peasant superstitions and the presence of the devil. The latter two traits are particularly suitable to Smerdyakov (and to Ivan's other devil, the one in his nightmare), insofar as Dostoevsky, like Gogol, derisively treats these "devils" as fools.

12. See Priscilla Meyer and Stephen Rudy, eds., *Dostoevsky and Gogol* (Ann Arbor, Mich.: Ardis, 1979). Nina Perlina's contention that Pushkin's is the most authoritative secular voice in *The Brothers Karamazov* (for which, see *Varieties of Poetic Utterance: Quotations in* The Brothers Karamazov [Lanham, Md.: University Press of America, 1985], 25) seems uncontestable. We do not subscribe to Victor Terras's claim that "[w]hile Dostoevsky loved and admired Pushkin, he never developed a similar deep feeling for Gogol" (Victor Terras, *A Karamazov Companion* [Madison: University of Wisconsin Press, 1981], 18). As we are arguing, Gogol is, after Pushkin, the strongest Russian literary presence in the novel.

13. Here we agree with Terras's intelligent observation: "The prosecutor is referring to the concluding passage of Gogol's *Dead Souls* (1842). He misquotes it (of course Gogol's passage does not say 'respectfully') and thus makes a travesty of it." Terras, *Karamazov Companion,* 18.

14. On the possible sexual latencies of the insect imagery in both writers, see Ralph E. Matlaw, "Recurrent Imagery in Dostoevskij," *Harvard Slavic Studies* 3 (1956): 201–25.

15. The translations from the *Iliad* are by Richmond Lattimore (Chicago and London: The University of Chicago Press, 1951).

16. F. T. Griffiths and S. J. Rabinowitz, "Tolstoy and Homer," *Comparative Literature* 35 (1983): 117–22.

17. Dostoevsky, as we know, began his career by "re-reading" seminal works of Gogol, by refashioning Gogol's Akakii Akakievich ("The Overcoat") and Major Kovalev ("The Nose") into the more emotionally complex characters of Makar Devushkin ("Poor Folk") and Yakov Petrovich Golyadkin ("The Double"). Nor are we surprised to find other standard Gogolian techniques throughout all of Dostoevsky's work, especially name symbolism. The very name of Dostoevsky's fictitious town "Skotoprigonevsk" ("Cattle Corral") has an absurdly Gogolian ring to it.

18. One of the most cogent and insightful statements regarding the mythic quality of *The Brothers Karamazov* is found in Proust's novel *The Captive*, from *Remembrance of Things Past:*

> But what a simple, sculptural notion it is, worthy of the most classical art, a frieze interrupted and resumed in which the theme of vengeance and expiation is unfolded in the crime of old Karamazov getting the poor simpleton with child, the mysterious, animal, unexplained impulse whereby the mother, herself unconsciously the instrument of an avenging destiny, a combination of resentment and physical gratitude towards her violator, comes to give birth to her child in old Karamazov's garden. This is the first episode, mysterious and grandiose, august, like the Creation of Woman in one of the sculptures of Orvieto. And as counterpart, the second episode more than twenty years later, the murder of old Karamazov, the infamy committed against the Karamazov family by the madwoman's son, Smerdiakov, followed shortly afterwards by another act as mysteriously sculpturesque and unexplained, of a beauty as obscure and natural as the childbirth in old Karamazov's garden, Smerdiakov hanging himself, his crime accomplished.

Marcel Proust, *Remembrance of Things Past*, vol. 3, *The Captive*, trans. C. K. Scott Moncrieff and Terence Kilmartin, and by Andreas Mayor (New York: Random House, 1981), 387. Originally published as *A la recherche du temps perdu*, vol. 6, *La Prisonnière* (Paris: Editions Gallimard, 1923).

19. Letter to N. A. Lyubimov, August 7, 1879, in *The Brothers Karamazov* (above, n. 1), 760.

20. Some have suggested a parallel between Dostoevsky's "confessional" and (largely) nonfictional *Diary of a Writer* and Gogol's similarly utopian *Selected Passages from Correspondence with Friends*. "In many respects Dostoevsky's word was as poisoned as Gogol's," claims Alex de Jonge. "The appalling jingoistic chauvinism of *Diary of a Writer* is his version of Gogol's *Selected Passages from Correspondence with Friends*." See Alex de Jonge, *Dostoevsky and the Age of Intensity* (New York: St. Martin's Press, 1975), 217.

21. [James] Michael Holquist, *Dostoevsky and the Novel* (Princeton, N.J.: Princeton University Press, 1977; rpt., Evanston, Ill.: Northwestern University Press, 1986), 175.

22. See René Girard, *Violence and the Sacred*, trans. Patrick Gregory (Baltimore: The Johns Hopkins University Press, 1977). Originally published as *Violence et le sacré* (Paris: B. Grasset, 1972).

23. A recent and insightful article that discusses Dostoevsky's novel as a story about the death of sons, wherein the father becomes the active agent and the child the recipient of his punishment, is Neil Bruss's "The Sons Karamazov: Dostoevsky's Characters as Freudian Transformations," *The Massachusetts Review* 26, no. 1 (Spring 1986): 40–67.

24. See Terras, *Karamazov Companion*, 443.

25. Dostoevsky's novel is not the only text to arrive finally at the beginning of the *Iliad*. The now lost *Cypria*, composed not long after the *Iliad*, did so to fill out the cycle of myths of the Trojan War. Apollonius Rhodius's *Argonautica* ends with the Argonauts sailing past Aulis, where their sons will launch the next great expedition. Jean Giraudoux's *La Guerre de Troie n'aura pas lieu* reimagines the preliminaries to the war as a critique of militarism.

26. Letter to M. M. Dostoevsky, February 22, 1854, in *Dostoevskii-Pisma*, 1:138–39.

27. Attila Fáj, *I Karamazov tra Poe e Vico: Genere poliziesco e concezione ciclica della storia nell'ultimo Dostoevskij*. Studi vichiani, vol. 16 (Naples: Guida editori, 1984). The allegory is summarized on pp. 97-101. Fáj discusses Dostoevsky's view of a final *ricorso* without reference to the final scenes (pp. 184–90).

28. Letter to M. M. Dostoevsky, January 1, 1840, in F. M. Dostoevskii, *Polnoe sobranie sochinenii v 30 tomakh*, vol. 28, pt. 1 (Leningrad: Nauka, 1985), 69.

WORKS CITED

Afanasev, Viktor, ed. *N. Gnedich, Stikhotvoreniya i poèmy.* Moscow, 1984.

Alter, Robert. *The Art of Biblical Narrative.* New York: Basic Books, 1981.

Annenkov, P. V. "N. V. Gogol' v Rime letom 1841 goda." In *Gogol' v vospominaniyakh sovremennikov,* edited by S. Mashinskii, 230–316. Moscow, 1952.

Asoyan, A. A. "Zametki o dantovskikh motivakh u Belinskogo i Gogolya." In *Dantovskie Chteniya 1985,* 104–19. Moscow: Nauka, 1985.

Aucouturier, Michel. "The Theory of the Novel in Russia in the 1930s: Lukács and Bakhtin." In *The Russian Novel from Pushkin to Pasternak,* edited by John Garrard, 227–40. New Haven and London: Yale University Press, 1983.

Auerbach, Erich. *Mimesis: The Representation of Reality in Western Literature.* Translated by Willard R. Trask. Princeton, N.J.: Princeton University Press, 1953. Reprint, 1974. Originally published as *Mimesis: dargestellte Wirklichkeit in der abendländischen Literatur.* Berne: A. Francke, 1946.

Bakhtin, Mikhail M. *The Dialogic Imagination.* Edited by Michael Holquist. Translated by Caryl Emerson and Michael Holquist. Austin: University of Texas Press, 1981.

Barolini, Teodolinda. *Dante's Poets: Textuality and Truth in the Comedy.* Princeton, N.J.: Princeton University Press, 1984.

Baroti, T. "Traditsiya Dante i povest' Gogolya 'Rim.'" *Studia Slavica Hungarica* 29 (1983): 171–83.

Belinsky, V. G. *Sobranie sochinenii v trekh tomakh.* Vol. 2. Moscow, 1948.

Belknap, Robert. *The Structure of* The Brothers Karamazov. The Hague: Mouton, 1967. Reprint. Evanston, Ill.: Northwestern University Press, 1989.

Benjamin, Walter. "The Storyteller." In *Illuminations.* Edited by Hannah Arendt, 83–109. Translated by Harry Zohn. New York: Schocken Books, 1969.

Bersani, Leo. "Against *Ulysses.*" *Raritan* 8, no. 2 (Fall 1988): 1–32.

Beye, Charles Rowan. *Epic and Romance in the* Argonautica *of Apollonius*. Literary Structures. Carbondale and Edwardsville: University of Southern Illinois Press, 1982.

Bitsilli, Pavel M. "Pochemu Dostoevskii ne napisal *Zhitie velikogo greshnika.*" In *O Dostoevskom. Sbornik statei*, edited by A. L. Bem, 149–54. Paris: AMGA Editions, 1986.

Bloom, Harold. *A Map of Misreading*. New York: Oxford University Press, 1975.

Bolgar, R. R. *The Classical Heritage and Its Beneficiaries*. Cambridge: Cambridge University Press, 1954.

Borghese, Daria. *Gogol a Roma*. Florence: Sansoni, n.d.

Bowie, E. L. "The Greek Novel." In *The Cambridge History of Classical Literature*. Vol. 1, *Greek Literature*, edited by P. E. Easterling and B. M. W. Knox, 683–99. Cambridge: Cambridge University Press, 1985. Reprinted, 1987.

Bowra, Cecil M. *From Virgil to Milton*. London: Macmillan and Co., 1945.

Branch, Watson G., ed. *Melville: The Critical Heritage*. London and Boston: Routledge and Kegan Paul, 1974.

Braun Maximilian. "*The Brothers Karamazov* as an Expository Novel." *Canadian-American Slavic Studies* 6 (1972): 199–208.

Brecht, Bertolt. *Brecht on Theater: The Development of an Aesthetic*. Translated by John Willet. London and New York: Harcourt, Brace, and World, 1964. Reprint, 1984. Translation with additional materials of *Schriften zum Theater*. Frankfurt: Suhrkamp Verlag, 1957.

Bruss, Neil. "The Sons Karamazov: Dostoevsky's Characters as Freudian Transformations." *The Massachusetts Review* 26, no. 1 (Spring 1986): 40–67.

Burgi, Richard. *A History of the Russian Hexameter*. Hamden, Conn.: The Shoe String Press, 1954.

Butler, Eliza Marian. *The Tyranny of Greece over Germany*. Cambridge: Cambridge University Press, 1935. Reprint, Boston: Beacon Press, 1958.

Cohen, Ralph. "On the Interrelations of Eighteenth-Century Literary Forms." In *New Approaches to Eighteenth-Century Literature*, edited by Phillip Harth, 33–78. New York and London: Columbia University Press, 1974.

Coleman, Robert. "Ovid and the Anti-Epic." Review of Brooks Otis, *Ovid as an Epic Poet*. In *Classical Review*, n.s. 17 (1967): 46–51.

Comparetti, Domenico. *Vergil in the Middle Ages*. Translated by E. F. M. Benecke. London: Swan Sonnenschein and Company; New York: Macmillan and Company, 1895. Originally published as *Virgilio nel medioevo*. Leghorn: Vigo, 1872.

Curtius, Ernst Robert. *European Literature and the Latin Middle Ages*. Translated by Willard R. Trask. Bollingen Series 36. Princeton, N.J.: Princeton University Press, 1953. Reprint, 1979. Originally published as *Europäische Literatur und lateinisches Mittelalter*. Bern: A. Francke AG Verlag, 1948.

de Jonge, Alex. *Dostoevsky and the Age of Intensity*. New York: St. Martin's Press, 1975.

Dostoevsky, Anna. *Dostoevsky-Reminiscences*. Translated by Beatrice Stillman. New York: Liveright, 1975. Originally published as *Vospominaniya*. Moscow, 1925.

Dostoevsky, Fyodor M. *The Brothers Karamazov*. Translated by Constance Garnett and Ralph Matlaw. Edited by Ralph Matlaw. A Norton Critical Edition. New York: W. W. Norton and Company, 1976.

———. *F. M. Dostoevskii-Pisma*. Edited by A. S. Dolinin. 4 vols. Moscow-Leningrad, 1928–59.

———. *Polnoe sobranie sochinenii v 30 tomakh*. Vol. 28, pt. 1. Leningrad: Nauka, 1985.

Driessen, Frederick Christoffel. *Gogol as Short Story Writer*. The Hague: Mouton, 1965.

DuRocher, Richard J. *Milton and Ovid*. Ithaca and London: Cornell University Press, 1985.

Egunov, A. N. "Lomonosov-perevodchik Gomera." In *Literaturnoe tvorchestvo M. V. Lomonosova*, edited by P. N. Berkov and I. Z. Serman, 197–218. Moscow-Leningrad, 1962.

Eikhenbaum, Boris. *Tolstoi in the Sixties*. Translated by Duffield White. Ann Arbor, Mich.: Ardis, 1982. *Lev Tolstoi, Kniga Vtoraya*. Leningrad, 1930.

Eisenstein, Sergei M. *The Film Sense*. Translated and edited by Jay Leyda. New York: Harcourt, Brace and Company, 1942.

Elley, Derek. *The Epic Film: Myth and History*. London: Routledge and Kegan Paul, 1984.

Erlich, Victor. *Gogol*. New Haven and London: Yale University Press, 1969.

Ershov, L. F. "Traditsii M. Sholokhova i roman-èpopeya v slavyanskikh stranakh." *Acta Litteraria Academiae Scientiarum Hungaricae* 28, nos. 3–4 (1986): 315–29.

Fáj, Attila. *I Karamazov tra Poe e Vico: Genere poliziesco e con-cezione ciclica della storia nell'ultimo Dostoevskij*. Studi vichiani, vol. 16. Naples: Guida editori, 1984.

Fanger, Donald. *The Creation of Nikolai Gogol*. Cambridge, Mass.: Harvard University Press, 1979.

———. *Dostoevsky and Romantic Realism*. Cambridge, Mass.: Harvard University Press, 1965.

———. "Influence and Tradition in the Russian Novel." In *The Russian Novel from Pushkin to Pasternak*, edited by John Garrard, 29–50. New Haven and London: Yale University Press, 1983.

Finch, Chauncey E. "Tolstoy as a Student of the Classics." *Classical Journal* 47 (1952): 205–10.

———. "Classical Influence on N. V. Gogol." *Classical Journal* 48 (1953): 291–96.

Foerster, Donal M. *The Fortunes of Epic Poetry: A Study in English and American Criticism 1750–1950*. Washington, D.C.: Catholic University Press, 1962.

Fowler, Alastair. "The Life and Death of Literary Forms." In *New Directions in Literary History*, edited by Ralph Cohen, 77–94. Baltimore: The Johns Hopkins University Press, 1974.

Fränkel, Hermann. *Early Greek Poetry and Philosophy*. Translated by Moses Hadas and James Willis. New York and London: Harcourt Brace Jovanovich, 1975. Originally published as *Dichtung und Philosophie des frühen Griechentums*. Munich: C. H. Beck'sche Verlagsbuchhandlung, 1962.

Freccero, John. "Dante's Ulysses: From Epic to Novel." In *Concepts of the Hero in the Middle Ages and the Renaissance*, edited by Norman T. Burns and Christopher J. Reagan, 101–19. Albany: SUNY Press, 1975. Reprinted in John Freccero, *Dante: The Poetics of Conversion*. Edited and with an introduction by Rachel Jacoff, 136–51. Cambridge, Mass.: Harvard University Press, 1986.

Gide, André. *Dostoevsky*. New York: New Directions, 1961. Originally published as *Dostoievsky: articles et causeries*. Paris: Plon, 1923.

Gippius, V. V. *Gogol*. Edited and translated by Robert A. Maguire. Ann Arbor, Mich.: Ardis, 1981.

Girard, René. *Violence and the Sacred*. Translated by Patrick Gregory. Baltimore: The Johns Hopkins University Press, 1977. Originally published as *Violence et le sacré*. Paris: B. Grasset, 1972.

Godard, Jean-Luc. *Godard on Godard.* Translated by Tom Milne. Edited by Jean Narboni and Tom Milne. New York and London: Viking, 1972. Reprint. New York: Da Capo Press, 1986. Originally published as *Jean-Luc Godard par Jean-Luc Godard.* Paris: B. Belfond, 1968.

Goethe, J. W. [von], and J. C. F. [von] Schiller. "Über epische und dramatische Dichtung." In *Goethes Werke,* edited by Erich Trunz. Hamburger Ausgabe in 14 Bänden. Vol. 12, pp. 249–51. 12th ed., 1981.

Gogol, Nikolai V. *Dead Souls.* Translated by Bernard Guilbert Guerney (as *Chichikov's Journeys: or, Home Life in Old Russia*). New York: The Readers Club, 1942.

———. *Dead Souls.* Translated by George Reavy. New York: W. W. Norton, 1971.

———. *Mirgorod.* Translated by David Magarshack. New York: Noonday, 1962.

———. *Nikolai Gogol: A Selection.* Translated by Christopher English. Moscow: Progress Publishers, 1981.

———. *"The Overcoat" and Other Tales of Good and Evil.* Translated by David Magarshack. New York: W. W. Norton and Company, 1965.

———. *Polnoe sobranie sochinenii.* 14 vols. Moscow, 1937–52.

———. *Selected Passages from Correspondence with Friends.* Translated by Jesse Zeldin. Nashville, Tenn.: Vanderbilt University Press, 1969.

———. *Sobranie sochinenii v semi tomakh.* 7 vols. Moscow, 1966–67.

Greene, Thomas. *The Descent from Heaven.* New Haven and London: Yale University Press, 1963.

Griffin, Jasper. *Homer on Life and Death.* Oxford: Clarendon Press, 1980. Reprint, 1983.

Griffiths, F. T., and S. J. Rabinowitz. "*Doctor Zhivago* and the Tradition of National Epic." *Comparative Literature* 32 (1980): 63–79.

———. "Tolstoy and Homer." *Comparative Literature* 35 (1983): 97–125.

Halliwell, Stephen. *Aristotle's Poetics.* Chapel Hill: The University of North Carolina Press, 1986.

Havelock, Eric A. *Preface to Plato.* Cambridge, Mass.: Harvard University Press, and Oxford: Basil Blackwell, 1963. Reprint. New York: Bantam, 1982.

Hegel, G. W. F. *The Philosophy of Fine Arts.* Translated by F. P. B. Osmaston. Vol. 4. London: G. Bell and Sons, 1920.

Holquist, James Michael. "The Burden of Prophecy: Gogol's Conception of Russia." *Review of National Literatures* 3, no. 1 (Spring 1972): 39–55.

———. *Dostoevsky and the Novel.* Princeton, N.J.: Princeton University Press, 1977; rpt., Evanston, Ill.: Northwestern University Press, 1986.

Homer, *The Iliad.* Translated by Richmond Lattimore. Chicago and London: The University of Chicago Press, 1951. Reprint, 1976.

Ivinskaya, Olga. *A Captive of Time.* Translated by Max Hayward. New York: Doubleday, 1978.

Jong, Alex de. *Dostoevsky and the Age of Intensity.* New York: St. Martin's Press, 1975.

Karlinsky, Simon. *The Sexual Labyrinth of Nikolai Gogol.* Cambridge, Mass.: Harvard University Press, 1976.

Kermode, Frank. *The Classic: Literary Images of Permanence and Change.* New York: Viking, 1975.

Kirk, Geoffrey S. *The Songs of Homer.* Cambridge: Cambridge University Press, 1962.

Koster, Severin. *Antike Epostheorien.* Palingenesia, vol. 5. Wiesbaden: Franz Steiner Verlag, 1970.

Kristeva, Julia. *Sēmeiōtikē: recherches pour une sémanalyse.* Collection "Tel Quel." Paris: Editions du Seuil, 1969.

Lamont, Rosette C. "Joseph Brodsky: A Poet's Classroom." *The Massachusetts Review* 15, no. 4 (Autumn 1974): 553–77.

Leavis, F. R. *The Great Tradition: George Eliot, Henry James, Joseph Conrad.* London: Chatto and Windus, 1950.

Lord, George deForest. *Heroic Mockery: Variations on Epic Themes from Homer to Joyce.* Newark: University of Delaware Press, 1977.

Lukács, Georg. *The Theory of the Novel.* Translated by Anna Bostock. Cambridge, Mass.: MIT Press, 1971. Originally published as *Die Theorie des Romans.* Berlin: P. Cassirer, 1920.

Macaulay, Thomas Babington. *Critical and Historical Essays Contributed to the Edinburgh Review.* Trevelyan Edition. Vol. 1. London: Longmans, Green, and Company, 1909.

McLean, Hugh. "Gogol and the Whirling Telescope." In *Russia: Essays in History and Literature,* edited by G. Lyman and M. Legters, 79–99. Leiden: Brill, 1972.

Madelénat, Daniel. *L' Epopée.* Paris: Presses universitaires de France, 1986.

Mann, Yurii. *Poètika Gogolya*. Moscow: Khudozhestvennaya Literatura, 1978.

Manzoni, Alessandro. *On the Historical Novel*. Translated by Sandra Bermann. Lincoln and London: The University of Nebraska Press, 1984. Originally published as *Del romanzo storico*. Milan, 1845.

Martz, Louis L. *Poet of Exile: A Study of Milton's Poetry*. New Haven and London: Yale University Press, 1980.

Matlaw, Ralph E. "Recurrent Imagery in Dostoevskij." *Harvard Slavic Studies* 3 (1956): 201–25.

Merchant, Paul. *The Epic*. The Critical Idiom, vol. 17. London: Methuen and Company, 1971. Reprint, 1979.

Meyer, Priscilla, and Stephen Rudy, eds. *Dostoevsky and Gogol*. Ann Arbor, Mich.: Ardis, 1979.

Morson, Gary Saul. *Hidden in Plain View: Narrative and Creative Potentials in* War and Peace. Stanford: Stanford University Press, 1987.

Nagy, Gregory. *The Best of the Achaeans*. Baltimore and London: The Johns Hopkins University Press, 1979. Reprint, 1981.

Nimis, Stephen A. *Narrative Semiotics in the Epic Tradition: The Simile*. Bloomington and Indianapolis: Indiana University Press, 1987.

Olson, Paul A. "The Epic and Great Plains Literature: Rølvaag, Cather, and Neihardt." *Prairie Schooner* 55 (1981): 263–85.

Otis, Brooks. *Ovid as an Epic Poet*. Cambridge: Cambridge University Press, 1966. 2d ed., 1970.

Parry, Adam. "The Language of Achilles." *Transactions and Proceedings of the American Philological Association* 87 (1956): 1–7. Reprinted in *The Language and Background of Homer: Some Recent Studies and Controversies*, selected and introduced by Geoffrey S. Kirk, 48–54. Cambridge: Heffer; New York: Barnes and Noble, 1964. Also reprinted in *Homer*, edited by Harold Bloom, 109–13. Modern Critical Views. New York: Chelsea House Publishers, 1986.

Pasternak, Boris. *Doctor Zhivago*. Prose translated by Max Hayward and Manya Harari. Poems translated by Bernard Guerney. New York: Pantheon, 1958. Reprint. New York: Bantam, 1985.

Peace, Richard. *The Enigma of Gogol*. Cambridge: Cambridge University Press, 1981.

Pedrotti, Louis. "The Architecture of Love in Gogol's *Rome*." *California Slavic Studies* 6 (1971): 17–27.

Perlina, Nina. *Varieties of Poetic Utterance: Quotations in* The Brothers Karamazov. Lanham, Md.: University Press of America, 1985.

Poggioli, Renato. "Gogol's 'Old-Fashioned Landowners': An Inverted Eclogue." *Indiana Slavic Studies* 3 (1963): 54–72.

Proffer, Carl. *The Simile and Gogol's* Dead Souls. The Hague: Mouton, 1967.

Proust, Marcel. *Remembrance of Things Past*. Vol. 3, *The Captive*. Translated by C. K. Scott Moncrieff and Terence Kilmartin, and by Andreas Mayor. New York: Random House, 1981. Originally published as *A la recherche du temps perdu*. Vol. 6, *La Prisonnière*. Paris: Editions Gallimard, 1923.

Pucci, Pietro. *Odysseus Polutropos: Intertextual Readings in the* Odyssey *and the* Iliad. Ithaca and London: Cornell University Press, 1987.

Ray, Robert. *A Certain Tendency of the Hollywood Cinema, 1930–1980*. Princeton, N.J.: Princeton University Press, 1985.

Redfield, James M. *Nature and Culture in the* Iliad: *The Tragedy of Hector*. Chicago and London: The University of Chicago Press, 1975.

Richter, Sigrid. "Rom und Gogol': Gogol's Romerlebnis und sein Fragment 'Rim.'" Dissertation, University of Hamburg, 1964.

Russo, Joseph, and Bennett Simon. "Homeric Psychology and the Oral Epic Tradition." *Journal of the History of Ideas* 29 (1968): 485–98.

Shapiro, Marianne. "Gogol and Dante." *Modern Language Studies* 17, no. 2 (Spring 1987): 37–54. Reprinted in Michael Shapiro and Marianne Shapiro, *Figuration in Verbal Art*, 191–211. Princeton, N.J.: Princeton University Press, 1988.

Simon, Bennett. *Mind and Madness in Ancient Greece: The Classical Roots of Modern Psychiatry*. Ithaca and London: Cornell University Press, 1978.

Simonsuuri, Kirsti. *Homer's Original Genius: Eighteenth-Century Notions of the Early Greek Epic (1688–1798)*. Cambridge: Cambridge University Press, 1979.

Stam, Robert. *Reflexivity in Film and Literature from Don Quixote to Jean-Luc Godard*. Studies in Cinema, vol. 31. Ann Arbor, Mich.: UMI Research Press, 1985.

Terras, Victor. *A Karamazov Companion*. Madison: University of Wisconsin Press, 1981.

Terz, Abram [Andrei Sinyavskii]. *V teni Gogolya*. London: Collins, 1975.

Tillyard, E. M. W. *The English Epic and Its Background*. New York: Oxford University Press, 1954.

———. *The Epic Strain in the English Novel*. London: Chatto and Windus, 1958.

Todorov, Tzvetan. *Mikhail Bakhtin: The Dialogical Principle*. Translated by Wlad Godzich. Theory and History of Literature, vol. 13. Minneapolis: University of Minnesota Press, 1980. Originally published as *Mikhail Bakhtine: le principe dialogique*. Paris: Editions du Seuil, 1981.

Tolstoy, Leo. *War and Peace*. Translated by George Gibian. A Norton Critical Edition. New York: W. W. Norton and Company, 1966.

———. *"What Is Art" and "Essays on Art."* Translated by Aylmer Maude. London: Oxford University Press, 1929.

Vermeule, Emily T. *Greece in the Bronze Age*. Chicago and London: The University of Chicago Press, 1964.

Veselovsky, A. "'Mertvye Dushi': Glava iz ètiuda o Gogole." *Vestnik Evropy* 3 (1891): 68–102.

Vogüé, E.-M. de. *The Russian Novel*. Translated by H. A. Sawyer. London: Chapman and Hall, 1913. Originally published as *Le Roman russe*. Paris, 1880.

Whitman, Cedric H. *Homer and the Homeric Tradition*. Cambridge, Mass.: Harvard University Press, 1958.

Yelistratova, Anna. *Nikolai Gogol and the West European Novel*. Translated by Christopher English. Moscow: Raduga Publishers, 1984. Originally published as *Nikolai Gogol i problemy zapadnoevropeiskogo romana*. Moscow, 1972.

INDEX